SUPERNATURAL
EXPERIENCES

SUPERNATURAL
EXPERIENCES

SID ROTH

DESTINY IMAGE® PUBLISHERS, INC.
P.O. Box 310, Shippensburg, PA 17257-0310

"Speaking to the Purposes of God for this Generation and for the Generations to Come."

This book and all other Destiny Image, Revival Press, MercyPlace, Fresh Bread, Destiny Image Fiction, and Treasure House books are available at Christian bookstores and distributors worldwide.

For a U.S. bookstore nearest you, call 1-800-722-6774.
For more information on foreign distributors, call 717-532-3040.
Or reach us on the Internet: www.destinyimage.com.

Trade Paper ISBN 13: 978-0-7684-3266-4
Hardcover ISBN 13: 978-0-7684-3483-5
Large Print ISBN 13: 978-0-7684-3484-2
Ebook ISBN 13: 978-0-7684-9099-2

For Worldwide Distribution, Printed in the U.S.A.

1 2 3 4 5 6 7 8 9 10 11 / 14 13 12 11 10

TABLE OF CONTENTS

	Introduction	7
Chapter One	Healed from a Brain-dead Coma (Richard Madison)	9
Chapter Two	The Finger of God (Darren Wilson)	29
Chapter Three	To Heaven and Back (Gary Wood)	53
Chapter Four	A Hug from Jesus (Bruce Van Natta)	69
Chapter Five	Supernatural Surgery (Jennifer Toledo)	85
Chapter Six	From Hell to Heaven (Earthquake Kelley)	101
Chapter Seven	Seeing the Invisible (Jonathan Welton)	123
Chapter Eight	A Radical Encounter with Jesus (Todd White)	139
Chapter Nine	Angels in the Night (Steven Brooks)	155
Chapter Ten	A New Reformation Is Coming (Jason Westerfield)	173

INTRODUCTION

We live in a world today where interest in spiritual things is at an all-time high. The materialistic and humanistic paradigms of the past no longer satisfy (if they ever did). More and more, people are curious about the supernatural; they want to *know* that there is more to life than just this physical existence. They yearn for the assurance that human life and consciousness extend beyond the visible realm.

Curiosity uninformed by knowledge, however, is dangerous and can lead to deception and error. The sharp rise of New Age and occult practices in recent years attests to this. If we are to explore and understand supernatural experiences, we must approach them with knowledge and wisdom laid on a solid foundation of truth. That truth is found in the Word of God, which says, "*The fear of the Lord is the **beginning** of knowledge, but fools despise wisdom and instruction*" (Prov. 1:7 NKJV, emphasis added).

For over 35 years I have researched and examined the divine encounters of hundreds of people, and I can affirm without hesitation that supernatural experiences *are* real. God *does* interact with people today and He often does so in direct and even miraculous ways.

But I have also found that as I draw close to God, He draws close to me! (See James 4:8.) As I develop intimacy with God, the supernatural becomes natural.

The Church should be at the very forefront in proclaiming the reality of supernatural encounters with God. Yet many Christians today have been taught that miracles, healings, and other supernatural experiences such as were common in the days of the apostles are not for today.

In the pages that follow you will meet ten people who are living proof that this is not the case. Their stories make it clear that supernatural experiences with the living, loving God are real and that they happen today. Some were healed of debilitating illness or crippling injuries; some received angelic visitations; some died and experienced visions of Heaven (and hell). One was delivered from New Age deception and another from a life of witchcraft and voodoo. Still another has traveled the world documenting divine miracles on film.

Ten very different people from very different walks of life, yet they share one thing in common: a supernatural experience with the living God that changed their lives completely. As you read their testimonies in their own words, you will be encouraged to believe that God can and does interact directly with people today. If it happened to them it can happen to you.

Chapter One

HEALED FROM A BRAIN-DEAD COMA

A head-on collision left Richard Madison with multiple broken bones and massive internal injuries. Initially pronounced dead on arrival at the hospital, he lay in a brain-dead coma for 27 days. Then, in response to the faithful prayers of Richard's mother and other family members and friends, God healed him miraculously and completely. Since that time, God has placed on Richard a powerful healing anointing. He has seen the blind receive their sight, deaf ears opened, and many people healed of various diseases. Richard has also seen 20 people wake up out of comas as of January 2010. Nine of these coma patients were brain dead. Along the way, he has learned that all believers can have this anointing in their homes and in their lives. If we learn how to receive, all of us who follow Messiah Yeshua (Jesus) can walk in this same anointing. Here is Richard's story.

Even before the life-changing accident where he was pronounced dead on arrival, Richard Madison was no stranger to close calls...

**...It was like the forces of evil tried
to snuff out his life early because they
knew he was destined to help many people.**

At the age of six months, Richard fell on his head and was in a coma for six days.

When Richard was five, a great uncle went on a rampage and shot Richard's grandmother five times. He would have shot Richard, too, except Richard escaped death by hiding under a bed. His uncle then left the house and killed himself. Miraculously, Richard's grandmother survived, brought back to life by the power of God.

A game of hide and seek nearly turned tragic when eight-year-old Richard hid from his cousin in a commercial clothes dryer. A young couple came in and discovered him there. The man held the dryer door closed and, ignoring Richard's screams and pounding, looked for change to start the dryer. Finally, the man's girlfriend persuaded him to let Richard out.

As a young man, Richard almost died from a cocaine overdose.

But the battle of all battles came a year later. On April 13, 1986, Richard had his closest brush with death in a traffic accident that should have killed him. Instead, it became the pivotal turning point in his life.

Dead on Arrival

Richard describes what happened:

The force of the impact in the head-on collision pushed my left leg into my pelvis, broke my left hip, and severely broke my right foot. Since I wasn't wearing a seatbelt, my upper body collided with the steering wheel, breaking most of the ribs in my chest. One of the broken ribs punctured the aorta artery at my heart while another one punctured my right lung. In addition, my spleen was ruptured, the C5 vertebra in my neck was broken, my jaw was broken, and my right eye was knocked out of its socket. Making matters worse, I was trapped in my vehicle. It took 39 minutes to get me out and transported to Vanderbilt University Hospital in Nashville, Tennessee, where I was pronounced dead on arrival.

Richard was declared dead on arrival and brain dead because his aorta had been torn and his spleen ruptured for 39 minutes. With such severe injuries and no brain activity, Richard's family was told to make funeral arrangements. Then circumstances took a different turn. Richard says the leading trauma physician later told him personally that he had been pronounced dead on arrival and was on the way to the morgue. In Richard's words:

Then the doctor said that something told him to bring me back and at least try something. When he said this I was stunned. I was still unable to speak, so I wrote the name "Jesus" on a piece of paper and showed it to him. He said, "I am not going to say it was Jesus that told me to bring you back," but I wanted the doctor to know that I knew it was Jesus.

It truly is amazing how God can use a few believers to accomplish His will. Richard had a lot of family members who went to church, but only a few really believed in miracles. When Richard first arrived at the hospital following his accident, he appeared to be beyond hope. Things did not look good for him that day, and his condition did not improve for the next four weeks.

They gave me 124 units of blood. I got hepatitis, yellow jaundice, blood poisoning, and double pneumonia. The doctors could not control the infections and fever. They put me in beds of ice to try to bring the fever down. They gave me every antibiotic known to man. My neck was in a brace because my C5 vertebra was broken. Since they did not expect me to survive anyway, they waited 25 days to repair my broken bones. All during this time I had no discernible activity in the lower lobes of my brain. I was in a brain-dead coma...

...the physicians advised my family to make funeral arrangements.

"You Don't Know the Power of My God"

For 27 days things were touch and go with Richard. He was kept on life support as his mother, aunt, and uncle stood firm on the Word of God, knowing that all things are possible to them who believe.

My mother refused to make funeral arrangements. She kept telling the hospital staff, "You don't know the power of my God." She brought any minister available in the ICU to lay hands on me, anoint me with oil, and pray the prayer of faith. I was unaware of anything going on. The doctors decided to repair my broken bones although I was still in a brain-dead coma. To their amazement, they discovered my neck was not broken anymore. The Holy Spirit had told my uncle two days earlier that my neck was healed.

They placed 3 steel plates, 19 screws, and 2 pins in my hip, foot, and jaw. During the surgery on my left hip, they accidentally severed the sciatic nerve. Then disaster occurred again. Two days after repairing the broken bones, my liver and kidneys stopped working. The doctors told my family there was no medicine available to make my liver and kidneys start working again. They said, "So far, we have kept him alive on life support, but you must sign the papers now because his organs have begun to shut down." But my mother said, "No, we are going again to the prayer room and pray until we hear from Heaven. My son shall live and not die."

Out-of-Body Experience

On the 27th day from the accident, I had an out-of-body experience. My family had just been told for the third time to make funeral arrangements because my organs had stopped functioning. Suddenly, I found myself walking through the hallway of a hospital, passing doctors and nurses. I walked right through them, but I couldn't feel them. They didn't even know I was there. I went into a room and saw my mother on her knees praying and calling on Jesus. I was not a believer in Jesus at the time of my accident. But as I watched my mother pray for me, I spoke to her. She looked in my direction and I knew something was wrong because she couldn't see me. She was praying for me and immediately I knew I had to do what she was doing. I looked up and said, "Jesus, if You are real, come on the scene and help me. Something is wrong." At that moment I felt a huge hand come down and cover the top of my head and heard a voice...

"I am Jesus, I am real, and I am going to raise you up and give you another chance."

Immediately, I was back in my own body. I woke up and reached for the nurse standing at the foot of my bed. She wasn't prepared for this any more than I was. During the previous ten-hour "death watch," I had swelled up, turned yellow, and started stinking from organ failure, infections, and poisons raging in my body. Four hundred staples from nine different surgeries were holding me together. I had 17 drain tubes and one feeding tube attached to me. My body had swollen as big as a barrel. My dad told me later that my head was as large as a basketball and that I smelled so bad that he had to hold his nose when he came in to see me.

When I sat up and reached for that nurse, I did not know where I was or how long I had been there, but I knew Jesus was real. I wanted to tell her about the hand, the voice, and the prayer room experience, but I could not speak because of the tube in my throat. When the nurse turned around and saw me reaching for her, she must have jumped about five feet. She saw a miracle right before her eyes as the swelling disappeared and I was awake. The infections left my body and I was no longer a vegetable, but I had a sound mind. The nurse summoned the doctors, and soon 12 of them stood at the foot of my bed asking me all kinds of questions. I communicated on paper, relating one miracle after another.

"Your Son Just Sat up Out of His Coma"

I was so excited that I wanted to speak out loud but I couldn't, and did not understand why. The doctors had performed a tracheotomy and my mouth was wired shut because of my broken jaw. The nurse realized that I was desperately trying to speak to her. She had seen with her own eyes that something extraordinary had happened to me, so she turned her paper over and said, 'What are you trying to say?' The ligaments had drawn up in my arms—it would take therapists several weeks to straighten them out—but I scribbled down as best I could, 'Is there a church here?'

She said, "You are at Vanderbilt University Hospital; you have been in an automobile accident. But I believe you are going to be okay now."

I wrote down on her paper that I had just come from a room that has red carpet, several pews and my mom and dad were there praying for me. I had never seen that prayer room before; in fact, I had never been in that hospital. Yet somehow, walking there in the invisible realm, I knew about the room and even the color of the carpet. I saw everything in detail. Reading my note, the nurse said, "There is a prayer room on the first floor, but your family is usually out in the waiting room." I scribbled down, "I know what it looks like, and I know my family is there. I just came from there."

That *really* shook her up. She motioned for another nurse to take my vital signs while she went downstairs to get my family. My mother told me later that a nurse walked into the prayer room and said, "Is there anyone here with a relative by the name of Richard Madison?" My mother stood up and said, "That's my son, but we are not making funeral arrangements. We are going to pray until Jesus raises him up." Then the nurse said…

"…you must be praying to the real God, because your son just sat up out of the coma and said he just came from here watching you all pray."

My mother and my aunt walked into my room holding each other by the arm. When they saw me sitting up, their knees buckled, and they began to weep. I heard them say, "I can't believe it! God really did it! I can't believe it! God really did it!"

Why was Richard's mother so confident that God would heal her son despite the massive nature of his injuries and the fact that initially he was pronounced dead on arrival? Richard says it was because of a vision she received.

> She went into the ladies room to wash her face and suddenly saw me in the mirror with a sheet over me. As she watched, the sheet dropped down until it looked more like a gown than a sheet. At that moment she believed that the Lord had revealed to her that He was going to raise me up and use me as a minister.

Instantly Delivered of Addictions

In addition to being healed of his massive internal injuries, Richard discovered also that the Lord had delivered him instantly from past and current addictions.

> None of the doctors could understand why I suddenly was awake or why I had a sound mind. For days I had been receiving large amounts of morphine for pain. One of the trauma physicians told me he was going to take me off the morphine gradually in order to prevent withdrawal. Still unable to speak, I wrote down, "Jesus raised me from the dead. I am not addicted to medicine." I didn't want any more cocaine, marijuana, or alcohol. So I just assumed that I did not need any more morphine. Jesus had set me free instantly. This was a

miracle, because I had wasted thousands of dollars on drugs and I did not need any drugs. Now the doctors wanted to give me drugs and I did not want any. God took the desire away. Even for cigarettes.

Five days later, the trauma physician came into my room and said, "Richard, I pronounced you dead on arrival. You shouldn't be here. You were a vegetable, yet now you have a sound mind. Your neck was broken. We had three x-rays showing it broken and now we have three more showing it not broken. We gave you large quantities of blood, and large quantities of morphine. I remember what you wrote on that paper about how you believe that Jesus raised you up and that you did not need any more medicine. Never in my medical profession have I ever seen anyone come off the amount of morphine that we gave you without being weaned off. There must be a God and He is watching over you."

"I Gave Away My Limp"

Even though God had healed him of his internal injuries and brought him back to life and soundness of mind from a brain-dead coma, Richard faced another challenge: learning to walk again. Because Richard had been brain dead, the doctors had not bothered to deal with his broken bones. Since they expected him to die, they did not feel that setting the fractures was a worthy investment of their time. Even with this, however, Richard experienced the miraculous.

The doctors waited 25 days to repair my broken bones. In the process they accidentally severed the sciatic nerve into my left leg. They also took three bones out of my right foot. They told me that I had a steel rod, 9 screws, and 2 pins in my left hip. I also had a steel rod and 9 screws in my right foot and I probably would never be able to walk again on my own. Perhaps in a year I might be able to walk with arm crutches.

Forty-nine days after the accident I left the hospital in a wheelchair. One day about eight weeks later I was praying. I was still a baby believer at that point and was still learning how to pray and how to use the name of Jesus. There was still a lot I did not know. I said, "Jesus, put feeling in my legs and I will get up and walk."

**Then I heard an audible voice,
a whisper. The Lord said,
"Arise and walk."**

I replied, "I know that is You, Jesus, but I can't walk; I don't have any feeling in my legs." He said, "You don't walk by feeling. You walk by faith." "How do you walk by faith?" I asked. "Just trust Me," He answered. "Stand up and walk." I trusted the voice of God. I knew it had to be Jesus because I also knew the enemy would never tell me I could walk. So I locked the wheels on the wheelchair and stood up.

Richard's doctor had warned him not to try to stand up because his weight would push the leg through the hip and destroy the right ankle. He was not supposed to do anything even as simple as pushing against the foot of the bed to scoot himself up. If he wanted to move, someone else had to move him. So why did Richard stand up that day and risk losing everything that had been accomplished? Because he wanted out of that wheelchair. Richard explains what happened next.

As I stood up I lost my balance and began to run. I ran through the living room trying to grab hold of something—anything—but there was nothing but open air. Finally, after running about thirty feet, I managed to stop myself by grabbing onto a door face. In amazement I said, "I just ran out of a wheelchair! Jesus, I will never doubt You again!" Then I looked around and realized I was about thirty feet from my wheelchair.

Needless to say, Richard's doctors were amazed to see him walking again. They never expected it.

A few weeks later I went back to the doctors. The orthopedic surgeon could not believe it when I walked into his office on my own two feet. At that time I was living with my aunt and uncle. They had rented me a walker because I still had trouble controlling my walking and they were tired of my weaving through the house, grabbing hold of them and nearly knocking them down. I used the walker for a week, then I began using a cane. It was with the help of that walking stick that I walked into the surgeon's office that day. Despite his amazement, he was concerned that I was going to break and destroy everything that had been accomplished. "You don't understand," I assured him, "this is Jesus. This is the power of God."

A few days later I picked up an elderly man hitchhiking on the side of the road and took him the 90 miles to his destination. As he prepared to get out of the car with his suitcase he looked at me with a sad expression and said, "I wish I had a walking stick. I left mine on the side of the road where you picked me up." Moved with compassion, I reached over and handed him mine and said, "I will get another one, so take mine."

About halfway home Hebrews 13:2 came to my mind. I grabbed my Bible and looked at the reference. *"Do not forget to entertain strangers, for by so doing some have unwittingly entertained angels"* (NKJV).

When I got home, I started chasing my aunt and uncle through the house to tell them about this man who could have been an angel. That is when I discovered that you can have a revelation from the Lord and nobody else gets excited about it. All of a sudden my aunt said, "Where is your walking stick? Why are you not limping anymore?" I looked down and said, "I gave my limp away." I never limped after that.

Richard's Life Today

Today Richard Madison operates in a powerful healing anointing. He prays for many people and has seen many healed as a result of his prayers. In particular, he has an anointing to pray for people in comas. Since being brought back to life from two brain-dead comas, Richard has prayed for 35 comatose people—20 have awakened. Nine of those were brain dead, but are now awake. He describes one such experience.

A man named Greg in Alabama was shot between the eyes. He was considered a vegetable, brain dead. The bullet went through his forehead and broke up into fragments. The doctor said it had scrambled his brain. I went to his home. His mother had been taking care of him, hoping and praying that something would happen. But after six months she was beginning to lose hope.

I went in and laid hands on him and prayed for him. I told his mother a little bit of my story of how the Lord had raised me up from my deathbed, and we just began to raise our hands and praise God. Then I said, "We are going to thank God for this miracle."

About a week and a half later I received a phone call. The lady on the other end sounded hysterical. I didn't know who she was, whether a friend or a relative. I finally got her calmed down enough to tell me that she was Greg's mother. She had called to tell me that Greg had just awakened out of this brain-dead coma even though the bullet fragments were still in his brain.

I have witnessed the power of Richard's healing anointing for myself. The wife of a friend of mine suffered a severe heart attack that left her in a coma. No one held out much hope for her recovery. I asked Richard to come and pray for her. He did. A few days later, she began responding to verbal commands. She woke up and kissed her husband and told him she loved him. Later, I asked Richard if he knew this would happen or whether he had simply prayed in faith. Here is what he said.

> I walked into the room and the Lord instructed me to put my hands upon her feet. Almost immediately I began to weep and I felt a strong anointing. After praying I told her husband Michael that I really believed the Lord was going to raise her up.

Expect the Unexpected

Richard Madison is an ordinary person who received a miraculous healing and a supernatural anointing to pray for the healing of others. But is such an anointing available to any believer? Can any follower of Messiah Yeshua walk in the realm of supernatural healing? Richard believes the answer to both questions is yes. One of the reasons so few believers do is because of shallow faith that confines God's supernatural work to a limited set of expectations and methods. The key to walking in the supernatural is to grab hold of a faith that looks beyond our normal perception of possibilities to God's unlimited abilities. As Richard says:

> I believe that the Lord wants His people to expect the unexpected. Anyone who believes can walk in this

same anointing. They can have it in their homes and in their everyday lives. He wants to help His people understand how to receive healing from others, how to expect to see others healed, how to speak the Word, how to stand on faith, and how to proclaim what they are believing God to do. There are so many ways to receive from God. One day it may work this way and another day it may work another way. We must learn not to place limits on what God will do. Fast, pray and speak the Word of God, and you will see the Glory of God manifested. Everyone has faith; you just have to use it. Hebrews 11:1 basically says that faith is thanking God for what you are asking, before you ever see it. Just simply ask, believe and receive!

Prayer of Impartation

Are you ready to receive an impartation of the same miracle anointing that rests on Richard's life? Are you ready to experience the supernatural experiences that he has experienced in his own life and as he has prayed for others? As you read these words and prayers, begin to turn the affection of your heart toward the presence of the Lord. Continue to focus on Him and feel His presence increase over your life.

Lord, we thank You for Your presence. We thank You for the supernatural experiences that You invite us into as a child of God. Thank You that You are hovering over us right now. God we ask that You teach us how to remove the limits that we've placed on You and to expect the unexpected. Reveal to us how to grab hold of a faith that is beyond our current perceptions of how You work and pushes us into the realm of Your unlimited abilities.

We stand upon Your word in Revelation 19:10 which says that, *"The testimony of Jesus is the spirit of Prophecy"* (NIV). We thank You for Richard's testimony of Jesus raising him from a brain-dead coma, and we believe that this testimony prophesies to us that You will do similar miraculous things in our lives. Lord, deepen our faith so that we take You out of the box and allow You to move in Your splendor and glory.

God, we love what You are doing, but we are so hungry for more. Lord, more! We are not satisfied with what we have experienced in the past. God take us to new levels in You. Let signs and wonders follow us who believe (see Mark 16:17). Empower us to raise the dead, heal the sick, and perform miracles in Your name and for Your glory. Help us lift Your name up so that all nations will be drawn to You (see John 12:32).

I am going to release an impartation of the healing anointing that is on Richard's life over your life.

In the name of Jesus, I release the healing anointing over every person who hears Richard's story. I declare that the heavens will remain open over you and that you will sense the thick and tangible presence of God over your life and body. I declare that you will hear the voice of the Father clearly and that healing will flow through your hands—the brain-dead will be healed, the dead will rise, the lame will walk, and you will have authority over all disease and affliction.

Like Elijah commanded dry bones to live, you will speak life into hopeless situations and miracles will take place at your command (see Ezek. 37:1-10). The anointing on your life will increase as you get older, and you will walk in greater miracles than even Jesus did (see John 14:12-13). You will be one who walks in great humility and gives all of the glory to Jesus.

Prayer for Healing

Maybe you know someone who is in a coma or who needs a healing touch from God. Now is the opportunity to exercise your faith and pray for them. Here is a prayer to get you started:

In the name of Jesus, I command life into this body. I speak to every cell, organ, and part of this body and declare that you are to live with abundant life in total healing and restoration. I speak the Zoe, quickening life of God over you and like Elijah commanded, I speak to the dry bones in your body and command them to live.

In the name of Jesus, I release the angels of Heaven to minister to your body and to release your healing touch. Father, I thank You that You are the God of miracles and that You are able to heal us. I praise You and lift You up for what You are about to do in this person's life. Thank You for this miracle.

For more information about Richard's ministry, please visit his Website at www.rickmadison.org.

Chapter Two

THE FINGER OF GOD

What happens when an evangelical Christian college professor receives a visit from an angel who tells him to make a film about miracles?

This is the unusual situation Darren Wilson found himself in. Why unusual? For one thing, an angelic visitation was the last thing he ever expected to experience. Furthermore, although he believed miracles were possible, he considered them to be fairly rare. He certainly had never witnessed one! In addition, he had never made a film before, and to top it off, he had no money for such a project.

Nevertheless, Darren Wilson traveled the world for two years, documenting miracle after miracle in dozens of countries, and the experience completely transformed his life. He gained an entirely new perspective on the love and power of God.

Your perspective will change too as you learn about gold teeth appearing out of thin air, an angelic visitation, people being raised from the dead, miracles, and mass salvations in the underground church in China, and entire Muslim villages being born again through the preaching of the gospel accompanied by miracles. This definitely is *not* your "old-time religion"! Read on and be transformed!

Darren Wilson is a professor at Judson University in Elgin, Illinois. He attended film school to become a screenwriter, never dreaming that one day he would actually be behind the camera himself making a film, especially a film about miracles. Why not? His conventional evangelical Christian upbringing, while allowing for the possibility of miracles, had very little expectation of seeing any. It took a miracle close to home to shake him out of that mind-set and awaken him to a higher dimension of God's activity in the world. Here is his description as presented in the introduction to his film, *The Finger of God:*

Darren: So what was the miracle that happened to you?

Woman: God gave us gold teeth.

Darren: Hold on. Did you hear that?

Woman: God gave us gold teeth.

Darren: I should probably stop it here and explain a few things. You are probably wondering who these people are. Well, I can assure you they aren't crazy. In fact, that's Aunt Patsy, and that's Uncle Bob. Now I'm not the type of person who believes everything he hears, but when your own family who you have known for your whole life and you know is on the up and up tells you that, well, this happened to them in church, let's just say it makes you start to question a few things.

So I began to wonder, "Well, if God put gold teeth in somebody's mouth, what else is He up to?" I decided to travel the world to find out. And let me tell you, if you think this is weird, it is about to get a whole lot weirder. Everyone, no matter who you are or what you believe has a kind of grid of understanding. Usually this grid is based on your experience or upbringing.

My grid was pretty simple: God can do miracles if He wants to, but I never saw any, so they must be pretty rare.

God was kind of like an invisible friend whose greatest hits happened a long time ago.

Back then, people needed raw displays of power because their theology wasn't as sophisticated as ours is now. There was one thing that I was pretty sure of: no matter what God did, He was very, very normal and He always made perfect sense.

Being new to all this miracle stuff, I figured the best place to start would be the one place that I knew best: church. So I started taking my camera to churches where I heard God was doing some, well, interesting things. I was already willing to accept the whole 'gold teeth' thing because of my aunt and uncle, even though I thought it was really stinking weird, but apparently God wanted to make sure I got the point.

It didn't take long for me to realize that gold teeth were just the tip of the iceberg. But even though so many people were getting these things, I couldn't shake that nagging question of 'Why?' Why teeth? Why would a God who is so normal do something so abnormal?"

With the sudden miraculous appearance of gold teeth, Darren Wilson found himself faced with a reality that defied everything he had been taught all his life to expect. In fact, had it happened to strangers rather than to close relatives he knew well, he would have dismissed it. He says, "If anyone other than my aunt and uncle had claimed to have received gold teeth I would have said that either they were lying or were misinformed." Instead, their experience set Darren on a whirlwind odyssey around the world to document the supernatural. But the miraculous appearance of gold teeth was just the beginning; the best was yet to come. As Darren says:

That is how it all started. As I moved out from that arena and around the world I began seeing people being literally healed in front of my eyes. For me, that is when it got *really* interesting.

"Are You Ready?"

Laying aside his ingrained skepticism of supernatural manifestations did not come either easily or naturally for Darren.

In fact, at first he resisted the Lord's prompting to make the film. It took an angelic visitation to overcome his reluctance. In his own words, here is what happened:

> The Lord had actually given me the idea for this movie about four or five months before and I didn't want anything to do with it. First of all, I didn't have any money. Second, I didn't have any contacts, and third, I didn't want to make an explicitly Christian movie. Those that were out there I thought were a little cheesy and inauthentic and I really didn't want to become a part of that. So I ran from it.
>
> In May of 2006 my father and my wife kind of "bribed" me to go to this church in Canada that was holding a big conference. I wasn't really interested but went anyway, basically just to make my wife happy. I must confess that at first I was very judgmental of everything that was going on. It was a very "charismatic" kind of thing. People were whooping and hollering and doing their little shimmy shakes or whatever you want to call it. Everybody, it seemed, was being wild and exuberant.
>
> On the last night of the conference I was standing in the back. Right in the middle of worship one of the speakers got up on stage and announced that an angel had just entered the room. The angel's name, he said, was "Breakthrough," and he had just come from Nigeria. He and all his angel buddies were there to minister to us, so we should just keep worshipping the Lord.
>
> I was in the back listening to all of this and thinking, "Yeah, right. There's an angel in the room now and

this guy happens to know his name and knows where he has been for the last ten years." There I was trying to worship while thinking all these unholy thoughts. I had my eyes closed like every good evangelical should, and as my eyes were closed I saw this thing pass in front of my eyes. You know how sometimes your eyes are closed but you can tell that somebody just walked in front of you? That's how it was here. Out of reflex I opened my eyes quickly, but there was nothing there. I closed them again and the figure was still standing there. I did not see a clearly defined being, but more like a shadow of an outline. He was crackling with an intensity I cannot describe, like a drill sergeant on ste-roids, really fired up.

He spoke to me and his voice rang in my ears. "Are you ready?" I had no idea what he was talking about. But because I had grown up in church…

…I understood enough to know that when an angel asks you a question you just say yes. So I said, "Yes."

And he said again, "Are you ready?" Again I said, "Yes." I could see his hands reaching up to grab my head, but I could not feel anything. He spoke a third time, screaming in my face, "Are you ready?" And I finally said, "Yes. Ready for what?" I still didn't know what he was talking about. He stopped and I felt his intense stare. Finally he said, "Make that movie."

He started to move away, and I called out in my head, "Wait!" This was the coolest thing that had ever happened to me and I didn't want it to end. As soon as I thought it he was back in front of me, but this time he was not intense anymore. Instead, he was the most gentle, loving individual that I have ever encountered. He was just oozing love. At this point I had absolutely no doubt that I was speaking with Breakthrough.

I saw his hand reaching for mine, and this time he spoke very softly. "What do you want? What do you need? I will stay with you all night if you need me to." And I said, "I don't need anything." I started blubbering. I really didn't need anything, but I just didn't want the experience to end. Finally I realized that he wasn't leaving. It occurred to me that perhaps he was waiting for me to release him, so I said, "Well, you can go now." Then he just drifted off. Immediately after this, the rest of my family got touched in their own way.

I came out of this encounter white as a ghost. My family asked me what was the matter, and I said, "Something just happened to me. I need to be alone for a little while." I went upstairs to a little balcony, sat down and began to pray. There the Lord just overwhelmed me with His love…

…It was the first time that I had ever felt the true weight of His love for me, and I was like a puddle on the floor.

Suddenly I heard Him say to me clearly, "Stand up." So I stood up and walked to the edge of the balcony. I looked down at all those people whom half an hour before I had been judging mercilessly. They were still doing their shimmy shakes and their whooping and hollering, but this time I saw them through the Father's eyes. I saw the brokenness and the hurt that were in them. Then I heard the Lord say to me very clearly, "Will you make it for them?"

"Yes," I said.

My only problem was that I had no budget; no money to make the film. So I made a deal with the Lord. "I will make this movie for You," I said, "but I don't want to have to ask anybody for money. If You will provide the money, I will make the film." I never asked anybody for a dime, but the Lord provided $25,000.

Dead Man Raised

Using the money God provided, Darren and his camera traveled all over the United States, into Canada, to Africa, Mozambique, Bulgaria, Turkey, France, Switzerland, and many other places. Everywhere he went he encountered—and documented on film—undeniable examples of the miraculous. One of the most amazing stories was that of Francis, a man Darren interviewed in Johannesburg, South Africa, while on his way to Mozambique. Francis had been beaten to death yet was raised to life again and instantly healed by the power of God. Darren describes the encounter:

> When I was scheduled to go to Mozambique I heard about a man named Francis who had an incredible story. I arranged to talk with him and he met me at the airport in Johannesburg during my layover. His story is simply mind-boggling.
>
> Two years earlier, during a church service, Francis was outside ushering people in. As he went to lock the gate, four men who were drunk came up to him. While he was trying to figure out what they wanted, they began beating him with baseball bats. "What are you doing?" he cried. They replied, "We are going to kill you. Today is your last day." They literally beat him to death. And as if that was not enough, they also stabbed him 27 times.
>
> Francis was taken to the hospital, where he was pronounced dead. The church heard about this and, not knowing what else they could do, started praying for him. Francis was killed around eleven o'clock at night. Around 12:15 or 12:30 in the morning, he came back to life. But when he came back to life he was a total

mess. Beaten to a pulp and stabbed 27 times, his face was swollen and he could not speak. The hospital staff gave him morphine for the pain and sedated him for the night. Just before he fell asleep, Francis managed to croak out in a whisper the words, "Forgive them," referring to his attackers. Then he was out.

Word of this got back to the church. Later that morning the police caught one of the attackers. The police were proud of themselves because in South Africa crimes of this type are rarely solved. The police contacted the church and said, "We caught one of the men who beat your friend to death. Come down and sign some papers, press charges, and we will get them processed." The church, however, knowing that Francis had already forgiven his attackers, said, "No, we are not going to press charges. We want to forgive them." The police were a little upset because in their view that was not really the best way to handle crime in South Africa. They continued to try to persuade the church to press charges. But the church spoke with one voice. "Absolutely not. We forgive him...."

**...and the moment they forgave
him as a church body, Francis was
instantly healed in the hospital.**

All of his cuts, all of his bruises, all the swelling—everything was gone instantly.

Two years later, Francis still had the bloody shirt he was wearing that day—complete with the 27 knife wounds.

Talking with Francis in the airport that day took my "grid" for the supernatural to a whole new level. It is one thing to hear stories about the miraculous; it is another thing entirely to look into the eyes of someone who has had an experience like this and know that this person isn't lying to you.

Miracles in China

Perhaps the most moving portion of *The Finger of God* is footage that Darren did not film himself, but was given to him by Dennis Balcombe, a 40-year veteran of missionary work among the Chinese people. As soon as he viewed the footage, Darren knew he had been given something extraordinary.

When I took a look at it, I knew I was sitting on something that was absolutely incredible. It is literally the rarest footage on the planet. It is culled from years and years of traveling around deep into the heart of that underground church. Watching it literally brought tears to my eyes because it showed me for the first time what heartfelt genuine faith really looks like.

The underground church in China is growing by leaps and bounds, and has been for many years, in spite of the repressive Communist government. The footage in Darren's film reveals part of the reason why. He describes several of the churches depicted in his film.

In one church the people wake up at 4:30 to come together for two hours to pray and worship. They do this *every day*. Another church meets in a cave, the only place where they are safe. Still another gathers on a farm far away from prying eyes. There is even one church where the people meet for twelve hours straight, even though the temperature in the building can reach 120 degrees. It is like this all over the country. There are over 3,000 house churches in the city of Shanghai alone.

One particular preacher was once crippled, but was healed when someone prayed for her. She now preaches the good news of Jesus to anyone who will listen. Another young woman, also now a preacher, was delivered from demon possession at the age of 18 by the ministry of Chinese Christians.

One particular meeting saw over one thousand people become Christians, while another church service was attended by over six thousand people. That may sound like a lot until you understand that this one church has over three hundred thousand members.

Often, Chinese underground churches start by getting everyone's attention using drama or music; then they pray for the sick. This has become common practice in the Chinese church and for good reason. As Dennis (Balcombe) put it, "I have seen AIDS patients completely delivered recently; a lot of different healings. And the healing and the miracles are one reason that many people come to the Lord."

One thing Dennis pointed out to me was that most of the underground churches in China are actually led by young people. These kids have all come out of the communist system and they want nothing to do with it. They only want to spread the love of Jesus to everybody they meet. The people are so hungry for the Lord and for His Word.

Dennis told me of a time he went to a very remote village in China to preach. He was led into a large room where the people were packed so close together that he had his back to the wall and still could reach out and touch the row in from of him. Everyone stood. There was no room to sit. He asked how long he should preach. They told him, "From 8:30 in the morning to 7:00 at night." Then they asked him, "If it isn't too much trouble, could you come back tomorrow and preach from 8:30 to 7:00 again?" And then very sheepishly they asked again, "If you would be so kind, could you come back the day after that and preach from 8:30 to 7:00?" He asked how often he should take breaks and they told him not to stop. The people would wait. When he asked them what he should preach on, they said, "Everything. From Genesis to Revelation." That's when it dawned on him that these people had no Bibles.

Are *you* hungry enough for God to get up at 4:30 *every* day for two hours of prayer and worship? Do you crave His Word enough to stand for 10½ hours straight for three days in a row just to hear it preached? The Christians of the underground church in China are, and that is why the church is growing exponentially there—and why miracles are commonplace.

The Glory Cloud

In the course of his travels for the film, Darren got linked up with Jason Westerfield, a man who walks regularly in the supernatural. (You will read Jason's story in Chapter 10.) They spent a day together on the Yale University campus, during which time Darren caught a glimpse of Jason's world. Darren describes his experience.

> While we were there Jason had a really powerful experience with the Lord. I was off to the side waiting patiently for him to finish so we could start filming. Afterwards, he related to me some of the things that he saw. I said, "Wow, that's pretty neat that you had that happen to you." Meanwhile, I was very bored. What happened next, Jason told me later, he did because the Lord told him to.

> Jason looked at me and asked, "Do you want to see into the spiritual realm?"

> "Sure," I replied. "Hit me with your best shot."

> "Take off your glasses," he instructed. I took them off. He placed his hands on my eyes and prayed a simple prayer: "Lord, open his eyes and let him see." With his hands still on my eyes he said to me, "Now Darren, when I take my hands off of your eyes you are going

to see into the spiritual realm, so don't get too freaked out."

"Okay," I said.

He took his hands off my eyes and said, "Now look up there between those two chimneys." When I looked, I saw with my bare eyes something that resembled sparkly firecrackers in the sky, like a fireworks display on the Fourth of July.

"What is that?" I asked in astonishment.

"It's the glory of God," Jason replied. "It's the glory realm of the supernatural."

All I could say was, "Holy cow!"

He pointed down the alleyway. The "firecrackers" were popping off even in the shadows. This whole experience was blowing my mind. Then Jason told me to turn around. We were standing in a huge courtyard which, five minutes earlier, had been completely clear. Now, behind us, half the courtyard was covered in a thick fog.

"What is that?" I asked.

"That is the glory cloud," Jason replied, "the cloud of God's presence."

This was absolutely the strangest thing that had ever happened to me. I was so shocked that even though I was holding my camera I never even thought to hit "Record." We walked out of the courtyard and hit the street. When I looked around, the cloud was following us. The whole street was covered in fog…

…when the angel commissioned me to document the supernatural I never expected to be living it; I thought I was only the messenger. But this was real.

With the glory cloud behind us, Jason said, "Well, God is here so now we can pretty much do whatever we want."

"Whatever we want" included healing a homeless man. It was midnight, the end of an amazing day. Darren describes what happened.

We were heading home when a homeless man approached us. He was the stereotypical homeless person; he smelled, he wouldn't look us in the eye, he had a limp, and he was asking for money. Jason told him he would give him some money but first he wanted to give him something better. First he prayed for the man's back, which the man had been complaining about. Then he prayed for his leg. While this was going on I just sat there and stared at this man. He had no one. He owned nothing. He was a homeless bum living on the streets. What was happening to him right now? What was God going to do to show him He loved this man? That is when I knew, beyond a shadow of a doubt, this man was going to be healed, not through anything Jason was doing, but through the love that God had for this man. He wasn't homeless; he was a prince. He wasn't broken; he was made whole.

And he was.

Before my very eyes this man's back and neck and leg were healed. Jason told him, "Those weights are gone. God healed you right here. God does work miracles. He loves you. God set you up tonight to be right here. You thought you were coming for silver and gold; some money, but the Lord said, 'Hey, I've got something better for you.' He will give you that, but He wanted to bless you tonight. You are His son; He loves you." This homeless man, who a few minutes earlier had come to us panhandling for money, was so excited over his healing that afterwards he forgot to ask us for any money.

"You Have to Love Them"

Another wonderful servant of God whom Darren encountered in his travels was a woman named Heidi Baker, who has a strategy to reach Mozambique, and in particular, the orphans of that country. She works with 7,000 orphans, but also reaches out to people of all ages, mostly Muslim, not only individually but also to entire villages, and with remarkable effectiveness.

Her secret? She is a person who, as Darren says, "exudes love." He relates two experiences he witnessed with Heidi, one in a Gypsy village in Turkey and the other in a Muslim village in Mozambique.

> We were in Istanbul, in a little Gypsy village. Heidi was with us, and there was a Muslim woman in the village who was blind in one eye. Heidi was trying to pray for healing in her eye, but she had to rely on a Turkish pastor as her interpreter, and he wanted the woman to get saved first. It was really interesting to me as a filmmaker to watch this dichotomy play out. On the one hand here was Heidi, freely offering love with no strings attached, no obligations.

...Her approach was to tell the woman, "God loves you. Let Him touch you and then you can decide for yourself."

> On the other hand was this well-intentioned pastor, who represented religion coming in and saying, "No, you have to become a part of our club first and then you will get your healing." It was fascinating to me to watch this back and forth between the two of them. Heidi kept saying to him, "You have to love them. You

have to love them." And he would come back with, "I do love her, but I need to train her first." He just didn't get it.

But that was Heidi, always overflowing with the love of Jesus. That was her life. She is one of the most loving people I have ever met."

An Entire Village Receives Jesus

On another trip with Heidi, in Mozambique, the event that transpired was so unexpected that Darren almost dropped his camera. He describes what happened.

This was the only time when I was filming that I almost dropped the camera, because I was not prepared for what took place. We had gone to a Muslim village which, like many that Heidi visits, had never heard the name of Jesus. In these situations Heidi often begins with some singing and dancing to get people's attention. Then she preaches for fifteen or twenty minutes, telling them about Jesus; who He is, that He is real, and what He has done and can do for them. At some point, she usually shows the *Jesus* film. Then she tells the people that she is going to prove that Jesus is real, and calls for the sick to be brought so she can pray for them.

On this particular occasion, Heidi had felt a strong sense from the Lord that there was a deaf woman in the village for whom she was to pray first. She was not to pray for anyone else until she had prayed for that deaf woman. For twenty minutes she called for this woman without a response. I was sitting there thinking, "Okay, she's not here. Let's move on." But Heidi was adamant; she was not going to pray for anybody else until she found this woman.

Finally, some of the villagers brought the woman forward. She had not been present; somebody had to go get her. I asked Heidi, "What took her so long to get up here?"

She gave me a strange look and replied, "She's deaf; she didn't hear me calling her."

"Oh." What more could I say?

The whole village testified that the woman truly was deaf. When she came up she had her newborn baby in her arms. Heidi began to pray for her and had some of the orphan children who were with us to pray for her.

And the woman could hear.

I have it on film. I remember holding the camera with tears streaming down my face. I have two small children myself. I was shaking. The other cameraman who was with us could barely hold his camera. He has children of his own too, and we were deeply moved at the realization that this woman was finally able to hear her baby cry for the first time. For the first time she would be able to hear her young child speak her name. I could hardly stand up. The presence of God was just so thick there. And once this happened, *the whole village came to know Jesus.*

What About You?

God commissioned Darren Wilson to make a film documenting the miraculous worldwide. Darren says the purpose of the film is to reveal what God is doing around the world and to show people that His love is not just a theory; it is a reality. He also acknowledges that making the film changed him forever.

This experience has changed my DNA, to be quite honest with you. It has changed me literally from the inside out.

It can change you too. There are at least three things Darren would want you to know as a result of his experience.

1. God is a God of *encounter.* He is actively pursuing a love relationship with you. He wants you to know Him in an intimate and deeply personal way. If you seek Him sincerely, you *will* find Him, because He has a glorious purpose for your life (see Jer. 29:11-14a).

2. God is a God of *extreme power.* He can meet all your needs and overcome all your difficulties. No challenge is too great for Him to handle (see Phil. 4:19).

3. God is a God of *extreme love.* He will never leave you or forsake you. Nothing can ever separate you from His love (see Rom. 8:35-39; Heb. 13:5).

Prayer of Impartation

Have you heard of miraculous healings or divine encounters and, like Darren, been skeptical? Or maybe you believe in miracles but have never seen them and long to.

If you want to see the world of the miraculous open up to you, pray this prayer with me:

Heavenly Father, forgive me for not always believing in Your miracles. I want to know You in Your fullness and see the ways that Heaven touches earth. Lord, open my spiritual eyes to see the ways that You are moving on earth today. Grant me the faith to believe in things that are outside the grid of my own experience. God, expand my grid!

Lord, I want to be a part of what You are doing on the earth today. I want to see the dead rise, the sick be healed, and to have supernatural encounters with Angels. Lord, take me past my skepticism and help me value spiritual experiences that I don't always understand with my mind. Like Darren, I want to be a puddle on the floor experiencing the awesomeness of Your love. I want to feel Your presence in a new and profound way. Lord, touch me.

I am going to pray a prayer of impartation over your life inviting you to experience supernatural things the way that Darren does.

In the name of Jesus, I release the anointing for divine encounters over you. I invite you into a supernatural odyssey that will change your life. You will see visions, dream dreams, participate in divine healings, and see evidence of Heaven's influence on the earth.

I release over you a spirit of Holy curiosity for what God is up to in the earth today. You will hunger for the supernatural in ways that you have never hungered before. Your desire to see God working and to partner with Him will be the driving motivation of your life. You will grow in your sensitivity to the Holy Spirit and you will walk in divine encounters.

I release over you a grace to steward the testimonies of Jesus, which will encourage the body of Messiah and win others to the Lord when you share them. I speak over you that you will keep a holy and godly perspective and not elevate the gifts and manifestations of the presence of God over the actual person of Jesus. In your quest to see the miraculous, you will not lose sight of your savior and friend.

I pray that the testimonies you witness and hear will become a spiritual legacy that you will pass on to your children, and to your children's children. The supernatural experiences that you have initially thought were rare and unusual will become so commonplace that your children will grow up believing that these things are normal. The spiritual breakthrough that you are reaching for will be the foundation that they build upon; your ceiling will be their floor.

I release you into a new season of God, one in which

you will be radically transformed and will testify of the goodness and faithfulness of God. Amen.

For information about Darren's ministry, please visit his Website at www.wanderlustproductions.net.

Chapter Three

TO HEAVEN AND BACK

Have you ever wondered what Heaven is like?

I have. My Jewish mother used to say, after she came to know the Messiah, "Heaven must be a wonderful place." When she died, my Jewish father had not received the Lord. Later, when he was on his deathbed, I remember saying to him, "Dad, don't you want to be with Mom? Remember, she used to say, 'Heaven must be a wonderful place.'" Then the Spirit of God moved on him and my Orthodox Jewish father received the Messiah. Today, Mom and Dad are together in that wonderful place called Heaven, waiting for me.

But what is Heaven like?

Gary Wood knows because he has been there. Gary died in an automobile accident and was transported to Heaven, where he witnessed many amazing sights. Among them was his best friend, decapitated in an accident on earth, now whole and fully restored in Heaven. But Gary did not remain in Heaven; he returned with a commission from the Lord to tell us about what he saw and heard there. His experience reveals that Heaven is more wonderful and more beautiful than we can possibly imagine.

Do you want to know what Heaven is like? Read on.

Life can change forever in the blink of an eye. That is what Gary Wood discovered on the night of December 23, 1966. Heaven was not on Gary's mind that night, but Christmas was. He remembers:

> I was driving home and my little sister was in the car with me. We were excited in anticipation of spending Christmas with our family. She was singing "Silent Night," and I was enjoying just listening to her beautiful soprano voice. All of a sudden she let out a blood-curdling scream. As I turned to see what was wrong, we crashed into the back of a 10-ton wrecker truck that was illegally parked on the edge of the highway. My sister had seen the reflection in the bumper and tried to warn me but it was too late. It was like crashing into a brick wall. Our car folded up like an accordion.

Miraculously, Gary's sister escaped serious injury. The same was not true for Gary. He felt pain, but not for long.

> At first I experienced pain; an explosion in my nose and a sharp, searing pain across the lower portion of my facial anatomy. Then suddenly I was relieved of all pain. Dying itself was completely painless. I remember a sensation of rising up out of my body. It was

like taking my clothes off and laying them aside. I was caught up in a massive, swirling, funnel-shaped cloud and engulfed in an extremely bright yet very tranquil light.

I began to rise upward quickly. It felt much like walking on one of those moving walkways you find at airports.

Suddenly I heard singing.

I know a little bit about singing. In high school I won several awards for singing, and at the time of the accident I was majoring in music at college. I had heard plenty of wonderful singing in my day, but this was the most stupendous singing I had ever heard in my life. The angels of heaven were singing: "Worthy is the Lamb that was slain to receive glory and power. Wisdom and dominion be given unto Thee forever, oh Lord. Amen and amen." Take it from me, you've never heard anything until you've heard trillions of angelic beings as they worship and magnify God.

The Heavenly City

If the singing Gary heard with his ears was glorious, it was matched by what he was about to see with his eyes.

As I marveled in the heavenly singing, all of a sudden the cloud around me opened up and I saw this gigantic golden satellite suspended in space.

...It struck me that the most stupendous thought that can occupy the mind of man is Heaven and how to get there.

Thank God that He has not left us to grope in the darkness but has given us His Word as a lamp to our feet and a light to our path (see Ps. 119:105)! The closer I got to the heavenly city—the New Jerusalem—the more I realized how perfectly it matched the description given in the Book of Revelation. It shone with a light like a jasper stone, crystal clear (see Rev. 21:11). Twelve foundation stones supported the city, and I remember seeing the names of the twelve apostles inscribed on them, one per stone (see Rev. 21:14). I also saw the twelve gates of solid pearl (see Rev. 21:21).

The Bible gives us the dimensions of the city.[1] A scientist who worked with me in Florida broke those dimensions down into some truly mind-boggling numbers.

1. Revelation 21:16 says, *"The city is laid out as a square; its length is as great as its breadth. And he measured the city with the reed: twelve thousand furlongs. Its length, breadth, and height are equal."* This distance translates to about 1,400 miles. The heavenly city, then, is 1,400 miles each in length, width, and height.

The heavenly city encompasses 2.7 billion cubic miles and is 780,000 stories high; enough room to comfortably accommodate a hundred-thousand-million people. That's more people than have ever lived on earth.

One of Gary's biggest surprises when he went to Heaven was being greeted by a familiar face, a departed friend sent especially to meet him and "show him around." Isn't that just like God, to send someone we know to welcome us? As Gary explains:

I learned that when you go to heaven, God has a special person assigned to you during the transition. It may be your mother, or some other departed loved one, but God has someone to 'acclimate' you, so to speak. In my case it was my best friend, who had been decapitated in an accident. Yet here he was again, whole and restored. I recognized him immediately. He looked exactly as I had remembered him on earth. We embraced and then just talked for a while. He said, "There are many things that I need to share with you," and then he took me on a tour of Heaven.

One of the things he showed me was my mansion. Jesus said, *In My Father's house are many mansions; if it were not so, I would have told you. I go to prepare a place for you"* (John 14:2). My mansion looked like a southern colonial home. It had a fence and beautiful marble columns. We walked inside and I saw three buckets of paint sitting in what looked like a living room area. My friend dipped his hand in one, threw it against the wall, and a beautiful floral arrangement appeared. People who know me would not be surprised when I say that I picked up the whole bucket and flung it against the wall. Suddenly the whole room was saturated with the fragrance of roses. "It's not ready for you to occupy," my friend said. "You've got to go."

We went back outside and I found myself walking on a street that was pure, solid gold. It was transparent; you could see all the way through it (see Rev. 21:21). Jewelers will tell you that there are impurities in gold that give gold its color. When those impurities are removed, gold is no longer yellow, but transparent.

Heavenly Library

Did you know that Heaven has a library? I didn't. But amazingly enough, it's true. Gary saw it and even went inside. He describes what he saw.

There were all kinds and volumes of books in there. When someone receives Jesus as his or her personal Lord and Savior here on earth, an angel will take a cloth and just wipe out all the sins and transgressions that person has done in life. That person's name is then written in the Lamb's Book of Life (see Rev. 3:5; 20:12; 21:27). In fact, I actually saw this happen. I saw a man on the earth receive Jesus, and then I saw an angel receive the report. He wiped out the transgressions of the man's life and wrote his name in the Book of Life.

> **...What was really precious to me was seeing my own name written in the Book. Next to it were the words, "Paid in full by the blood of Jesus."**

I saw other books there as well: books with prayer requests in them; books that record our spiritual growth here on earth; even a book recording the names of souls that each of us as Christian believers have won to the Lord.

There were all kinds of books besides these in the library, which shows me that in heaven we all will be continually learning. Our learning experiences will not end when we depart this earth; they will continue in Heaven.

Leaving the library, I witnessed many other awe-inspiring things. I saw the seven golden lamps that represent the Holy Spirit (see Rev. 4:5). I saw God's throne, with 24 elders seated around it (see Rev. 4:4). I saw one room that was labeled "Unclaimed Blessings." When I opened the door I saw legs, I saw arms, I saw every portion of one's anatomy. People often ask me why there is a room like that in Heaven. Because God has a spare parts room. He has miracles of healing and restoration ready for the asking. As a matter of fact, I saw people on earth pray and request a miracle. I saw the prayer request go up, I saw the angels go get the prayer request, and I saw them go back down. But I also heard some people say, "The day of miracles has passed," and "There never was a day of miracles." They are wrong. The day of miracles has *not* passed. There *is* a God of miracles, and He has a miracle for you right now.

Heavenly Healing

Gary's own miracle was about to come. As much as he would have liked to stay in Heaven, it wasn't his time yet. He returned to earth and to his body with a commission from God, and his return demonstrates the power of prayer. As Gary explains:

I didn't want to return. When you're over there in that realm, you realize that it is far better than life on this earth. Even now, so many years later, I sometimes get that faraway look in my eye and kind of "zone out," prompting my wife Deena to say, "Earth to Gary, earth to Gary." But I did return, and I did so because my little sister began to pray the name of Jesus. His is the most powerful name on the face of the earth. She had heard the doctors pronounce me dead, so she began praying with all her heart.

From my vantage point in Heaven I was able to see what happens on that end when the children of God pray. Every angel stands at alert. They immediately stop whatever they are doing and draw their swords, ready to be summoned and sent to hearken to the voice of the child of God who uses the precious name of Jesus. I even saw demon forces tremble whenever a believer prayed in the name of Jesus.

As a result of the prayers of Gary's sister, his tour of Heaven ended and he returned to his body. He came back to life. But he was not out of the woods yet. He had suffered horrific injuries in the accident.

They rushed me to San Juan County Medical Hospital in Farmington, New Mexico, and did an evaluation. The turn signal indicator had sliced my nose off. I had to have 100 stitches in my face. Both my jaw and my neck were broken in three places. My vocal cords and larynx were crushed. The doctors said I would never be able to sing again. It seemed they were right. I couldn't even speak, let alone sing.

A crushed larynx is a serious injury. It's not like you can get a transplant as you could for a kidney. There is no operation to replace a crushed larynx; nothing that medical science can do. Yet Gary was completely healed. How? It happened one day in the hospital when he was worshiping God. He relates what took place.

I was listening to the song "He Touched Me" by Bill Gaither on the radio, and said in my spirit (since I couldn't speak), "God, You can touch me. You can do what this says. With God nothing is impossible."

**...At that moment Jesus walked
into my hospital room. I saw
Him just like I had seen Him in
Heaven. *And He touched me.***

Right after this the nurse walked in and said, 'Good morning, Mr. Wood. How are you doing?' She'd been doing this for the last nine months. Her job, of course, was to encourage me, cheer me up, and try to keep me from becoming depressed.

When Jesus comes into the room, everything changes. I threw my hands up in the air and said, "Praise God, I've been healed!"

She dropped her tray in astonishment and went running for the doctor. They examined me thoroughly and couldn't understand. By all accounts I should not have been able to talk at all. But I got a second opinion. Doctor Jesus healed me, and I've been going everywhere telling everyone. Physically, my larynx still was not "healed": it was still crushed. Yet I was able to talk. The only explanation is the supernatural, miracle working power of God. I believe in miracles. God is a miracle worker. Job 37:14 says, *"Stand still and consider the wondrous works of God"* (KJV). He performed this miracle on my behalf, and He wants to perform miracles in people's lives today.

Not long after this, Gary and some of his friends experienced God's miracle-working power in an amazing way that involved a heart attack, another out-of-body experience, and, incredibly, the apparent stoppage of time itself. Gary describes what happened.

I went to a home to lead a Bible study and one of the words of knowledge that I received was that someone had suffered a heart attack. There was no apparent or immediate verification of this, so after the study was over we left. After we had ridden for a little bit one of the ladies realized she had forgotten her purse, so we turned around and went back. When we arrived at the house we saw an ambulance in front. In the time since we had left shortly before, the man of the house had suffered a massive heart attack and died. But he came back to life. "I've just been to Heaven," he told everyone there, "and the Lord Jesus told me that everything Gary is saying is true."

With that, everyone wanted me to pray for them. We were there for another 45 minutes. Here is where the story really becomes remarkable, so much so that sometimes I hesitate even to tell it. Yet six people verified what happened, one being my wife. When we left the house originally, the time was 10:30 p.m. We drove for a little while, returned for the one lady's purse, learned of the heart attack and the return to life of the victim, and spent 45 minutes praying for people. As we left to return home for the second time, we glanced at the car clock and we all gasped in amazement. The time was...*10:30 p.m.* God had stopped time to verify this word of knowledge for this brother. Today he is healthy, whole, and well and serving God. Isn't God amazing?

A Heavenly Message

Gary Wood was severely injured—and even died—in an automobile accident, but his trip to Heaven was no accident. God has a purpose for everything He does. His purpose in bringing Gary to Heaven was to send him back with a message for the rest of us. Gary has written about it in his book, *A Place Called Heaven*. Here is a brief summary, in Gary's own words.

God told me to make Him real to people of this earth. He sent me back with a message focusing on three specific areas; three specific things we are to look for in the days ahead.

1. A spirit of restoration that will prevail throughout the land. Get ready for prodigals to return.

2. A spirit of prayer will arise. The Lord showed me how to pray. He told me to pray, "It is written"; then I could claim, "It is finished." He showed me demonic spirits over cities and how to bombard heaven and get prayers released and receive answers.

3. Miracles will increase; miracles unprecedented in time and eternity, such as mankind has never seen before. All three of these things taking place

simultaneously will be a dramatic sign of the Messiah's imminent return.

I want you to know that God really loves you. You are very special to Him, and He wants to give you a miracle. All you have to do is have faith—*believe.* God has a miracle with your name on it. Claim it and receive it; believe and receive, and He'll give you your miracle.

The God who can stop time can do anything. During his visit to Heaven, Gary went into the library and saw the Book of Life. I have a question for you: *Is your name written there?* Or does the library of Heaven still hold the record of all your sins and transgressions? Would you like to know that every bad thing you've ever done has been washed away by the blood of Jesus so your name can be in the Book of Life? I urge you to get right with God. The Bible says that today is the day of salvation. Do not miss this moment of your visitation. Repent. Tell God you're sorry for your sin. Believe that the blood of Jesus washes away all your sins. Ask for the power to overcome these sins. Make Jesus your Messiah and ask Him to live inside of you.

...Grab a Scripture. Hold on for dear life, and guess what? It's yours.

By His stripes you *were* healed. You *were* healed. By His stripes—by His sacrifice—the blood came that washes away our sin and heals all our diseases. Agree with the promises of God's Word and your name will be inscribed in the Book of Life.

Prayer of Impartation

Gary's testimony of visiting Heaven is so incredible. He allowed what he saw to alter his faith. While lying in the hospital with a crushed larynx, he declared that nothing is impossible with God. This faith-filled statement opened the realm of the supernatural to Gary. The equation changed, and Jesus walked into the room.

You can allow these testimonies to alter your faith. Testimonies can build a "grid of understanding" that will attract the miraculous to you.

Father, I pray a release of the Glory of God over each person reading Gary's story. I pray that their minds would be transformed to discern how You are moving in the earth today.

I pray that these believers will stand on these supernatural testimonies and declare that You can and will do the same for them.

I release over everyone reading this book the anointing that is on Gary's life—to show the world that God is real. I pray that you would catch this spirit of prayer that Gary talks about and be a forerunner in the realm of encountering the supernatural. I pray that your testimonies would, in turn, build a grid for the supernatural in the lives of others.

I pray that the miracles that you are a part of would be even greater than those that Gary is a part of. I pray that your faith and courage would exponentially grow and that you would obey God in out-of-the-box ways.

I release over you the gift of words of knowledge and divine healing. You will begin to hear God's voice more and more clearly, and you will see the sick healed when you pray. Your life **will** make a difference for the Kingdom.

I pray that you would become a lightning rod for miracles and that the heavenly activity on earth would be attracted to you. I release great faith and boldness over you to stand in the gap for others who need divine healing.

When others have little faith, you will rise up and declare that God is good, faithful, and a healer.

I declare that you have access to the spare parts room that Gary saw in Heaven. When you pray for healing on earth, angels will be commissioned to carry out the miracle and it will be done on earth as it is done in Heaven. I pray that God gives you revelatory insight into what else is in the unclaimed blessings room so that you may lay hold of it.

Prayer for Healing

If you need healing while you are reading this, I speak divine healing over your body. I speak life into every cell, nerve, muscle, and organ. I command disease and death to leave your body and to never return. I speak total and complete restoration over you physically and emotionally, and declare that you have been sealed with the Holy Spirit so that this sickness can never return (see 2 Cor. 1:22; Eph. 1:13). Amen.

For further information about Gary's ministry, please visit his Website at www.garywood-ministries.org.

Chapter Four

A HUG FROM JESUS

Bruce Van Natta is an ordinary man who hears God's voice. At the age of five, he had a supernatural encounter with Jesus, who came into his room one night, gave him a hug, and imparted spiritual gifts to him. Not long after this, Bruce had a dream of walking and talking with Jesus in Heaven. Years later, as an adult, he nearly died when an eight-ton logging truck fell on his stomach. The axle crushed him like a pancake. He literally thought he was cut in two. Bruce surely would have died except that two angels appeared out of nowhere and miraculously saved his life.

Bruce hears God speak to him every day. He wants you to know that you too can begin hearing God's voice and receive God's direction for your life. You will be both encouraged and inspired as you read Bruce's remarkable story.

Five years old is a young age to begin operating in the things of the Spirit of God, but that is exactly what happened to Bruce Van Natta. It all started with a hug from Jesus in the middle of the night in answer to a prayer prayed by a frightened, hurting little boy. Bruce remembers that night.

Both my parents worked away from home, so I stayed at a babysitter's house each day while they were gone. The parents in this home were molesting their two children, and over the year or so that I stayed with them they also molested me.

One Sunday my grandparents took me to church, the one time I can remember being in church as a small child. It was a little country church. I went to a Sunday school class and the teacher told us a story about Jesus hugging little children (see Mark 10:13-16). His main point was that Jesus loved us as children, and if we would pray to Him, He would answer our prayers.

Fortunately, my parents found out what had been happening to me at the babysitter's house and took me out of that situation. But they were worried about me. One night I lay in bed listening to their conversation. They were upset that I had never said anything and worried about how this experience would affect me in the future.

As I lay on the bed in the dark, a little voice inside, which I know now was the Holy Spirit, reminded me of what the Sunday school teacher had said six months earlier. Then the voice said to me, "Pray to Jesus." I decided to give it a chance. What I wanted more than anything else at that moment was what I think any child that age and in my situation would have wanted: to be comforted...

...so I prayed for a hug. That's all. I said, "Jesus, please come hug me."

At that very second the room lit up and I felt warm arms wrapped physically around me. The experience was both physical and emotional. I felt like I had been dipped in liquid love. It covered me from head to toe, filled me inside and out, and blocked out everything else. The next thing I knew, I was waking up the next morning.

Bruce did not realize it at the time, but he had received an impartation of spiritual gifts. Not long after his "hug" in the night, he had another supernatural encounter. As he recalls:

Shortly after that, I had a dream where I was walking in Heaven hand in hand with Jesus. The walls were made of beautiful jewels and the road we were walking on was very shiny. We didn't talk; Jesus just smiled at me and held my hand as we walked. I felt embraced by love. Later, I told my mom about it. She knew from the Book of Revelation something of what Heaven looks like. Even though I had no prior knowledge of it, I described it and it scared her a little.

All I really remember seeing were these beautiful stone walls. When we think of diamonds, we usually think of little stones. The stones I saw were huge and beautiful. To this day, I still have a fascination with stones. I even have a stone garden at home. I think my interest in stones stems from that dream of Heaven. From that point I began to have many dreams and visions, as well as what the Bible calls words of knowledge.

Touched by Angels

As so often happens, it was a routine, normal day, like so many others, when disaster struck suddenly and without warning. But disaster quickly became miracle. Bruce will never forget that day.

I was a mechanic by trade. I owned my own repair truck and did on-site repairs at different locations. When the accident occurred I was just finishing up a three-day job. That day I had put in about twelve hours. I had done an engine repair but wanted to run the engine to make sure there were no leaks on any of my repair work. Another mechanic was working with me to make the job go faster. It was a Peterbilt logging truck, empty weight around 16,000 pounds. He had taken the right front wheel off and jacked up the front axle with a 20-ton bottle jack.

As I was wiping my tools off and putting them in my truck, he asked me, "Before you go, can you take a look at something? I've got a leak somewhere in this truck that I've been trying to find for six months. If you can just diagnose it, I'll fix it myself."

I thought to myself, "That should only take a couple of minutes." His creeper and his light were right there. I had not been underneath the truck once on this job, but now I crawled up underneath it feet first so that my feet were towards the back of the truck. The two front wheels normally carry 10,000 to 12,000 pounds of the truck weight, but one wheel was off, replaced by a jack. The front axle was broad, deep, and somewhat rounded. As I crawled underneath the truck to begin my inspection, the front axle was right above my midsection. The vibration of the running engine caused the truck to rock in such a way that it fell off the jack. That rounded axle fell across my midsection and crushed me like a blunt guillotine. It didn't cut me, but crushed me down to the thickness of my spine. Two of my lumbar vertebrae were broken, along with a couple of ribs. All of my internal abdominal organs really took a hit, particularly my intestines, but also my spleen, pancreas, and liver.

Immediately after that axle came down I was still conscious. I looked at myself and from my point of view it looked like I was cut in half because I could not see the lower half of my body. All I could see was that axle lying on the concrete floor. "God, help me!" I called out. Then I said it again: "God, help me!"

The mechanic working with me was quick to act. He called 911 then worked to get the truck jacked up again.

I remember *really* wanting to get out from underneath that truck because I didn't like the way it was jacked up and was afraid it would fall on me again. Reaching back I managed to grab hold of the truck's big chrome front bumper, which was right behind my head, and pulled myself out to the point where my head was sticking out from underneath the bumper. At that point I lost consciousness. The next thing I knew, I was up at the ceiling of the garage looking down on the whole scene. I didn't feel anything. It was like watching a movie. More people arrived—EMTs from the local volunteer fire department—and I could hear the conversations they were having...

...this whole out-of-body experience was incredible, especially the sensation of looking down at myself.

I was lying there under the front bumper, my eyes closed and my head turned to the right.

But the most incredible thing I saw from my overhead perspective was the sight of two huge glowing angels kneeling on either side of me. The man I had been working with was running his fingers through my hair, crying, and patting me on the head. He was a big man, easily 6' 1" or 6' 2", but the two angels were at least head and shoulders taller than he was. Their arms were underneath the truck, and although I could not see them, I knew their hands were on me, keeping me alive.

The rescue team pulled me out from underneath the truck. The angels stayed. I watched as a red-haired first responder named Shannon—I met her later—came in from the back corner of the garage. She moved my co-worker out of the way, knelt down between the two angels, and started slapping me in the face, saying, "Open your eyes; open your eyes." I was watching from above, listening to her, and suddenly the next thing I knew I was back in my body, looking at her eye to eye.

Two Miracles

Due to the grievous nature of Bruce's injuries, the first responders called immediately for a med-evac aircraft, which airlifted Bruce to the largest trauma center in the state of Wisconsin. It was a miracle he even made it, because by all accounts, he should have been dead by the time help arrived. This, in fact, was the first of two miracles for Bruce that enabled him to escape death. He explains:

The doctors told me that because of the severity of my injuries, I should have bled to death. My superior mesenteric artery and superior mesenteric vein, which circulate blood through the lower half of the body, had both been severed in multiple places. Not just pinched or torn, but completely severed. We're talking about an artery and a vein with very large diameters being cut completely in two. Other more secondary blood vessels had been severed also. They said that with my injuries I should have bled to death in 8 to 10 minutes *at most*. In fact, several doctors told me that they could find no other cases anywhere of anybody ever living from injuries such as mine. They always came in dead on arrival.

Everyone at the trauma center who worked on me was amazed that I survived. One hour and 40 minutes elapsed from the time of the accident to the time I arrived at the hospital. I had been in the trauma unit for an hour when I lost all blood pressure and they rushed me into the OR. I should have lost all blood pressure in those first 8 to 10 minutes after the accident. My medical records indicate that I was given 18 units of blood, which is about 8 liters. The human body holds about 5 to 6 liters, which indicates that as soon as they gave me blood it leaked into my stomach cavity. So it truly was a miracle that I even made it to the hospital alive.

Severe blood loss from severed arteries and veins was not the only life-threatening part of Bruce's injuries. His small intestine was ravaged so severely that it was almost destroyed. But this injury set the stage for miracle number two. Bruce continues with his story:

My small intestine was damaged so badly that they were able to save only a 25-centimeter, or 10-inch, chunk of the ileum. They had to cut away three large sections of intestine that were too damaged to save, but salvaged a second piece that was about 75 centimeters long, which they surgically attached to the other. Between those two pieces, I had roughly 100 centimeters of small intestine left, or about 3 feet. Adults normally have 21 to 22 feet of small intestine, and here I was with only 3 feet left. As a result, I started to lose weight while I was in the hospital. Then things got worse. I went through five different operations. The fourth operation was to remove a portion of the 75-centimeter length of intestine that had died. Now I had less than 100 centimeters of small intestine, and I kept losing weight.

The danger with this is that a person with small bowel syndrome or, as in my case, an insufficient amount of small intestine, will inevitably starve to death if the amount of intestine drops below a certain point. And I was below that point. Even though I was being fed intravenously, I was slowly dying.

One morning right after I had come out of my fourth operation, a man named Bruce Carlson showed up in my room. He was from New York and told me that the Lord had awakened him two mornings in a row and told him to fly to Wisconsin and pray over me. Bruce was a friend of a friend; I had met him once before while on vacation. He walked in with two friends from my church who had driven him to the hospital. One of them stood at the foot of the bed while Bruce and the other friend prayed from each side. He placed his palm on my forehead and prayed, "Lord, I ask that all the prayers of all the people that have been praying for

Bruce be answered right now, today." I was on prayer chains all over.

As Bruce Carlson was praying, I felt what I can describe only as electricity come out of his palm and into my forehead. Then, just as Jesus spoke to the mountain, Bruce said, "Small intestine, in the name of Jesus, I command you to grow supernaturally in length right now!" As soon as he said that, it felt like a snake came uncoiled inside my stomach.

Bruce was not imagining things. Something miraculous happened that day, as subsequent radiological examinations bore out.

In preparation for operation number five a few months later, I went to the radiology department to have an upper GI. They made me drink this nasty stuff, a radioactive dye, and then they measured it from the bottom of my esophagus, checking my small intestine. The technician obviously was puzzled by the result because I heard him say, "Hmm," and then he went to get his supervisor. They redid the test and I heard them whispering together. I caught the word "mistake." That's the *last* thing you want to hear a doctor say! So I asked about it, and he said, "No, it's good. Your records show that you have less than 100 centimeters of small intestine, but we've just done the test twice and you have **well over** 200 centimeters."

Was it a fluke? A mistake in the records? A bad diagnosis? Bruce is convinced otherwise. As he explains:

We later were told by the senior radiologist that there was at least 9 feet of small intestine now. Considering that there was a team of doctors, and the doctor who headed up the operations was the head of the biggest trauma center in our state, as well as being a renowned surgeon, I don't think it was a mistake in the records or a bad diagnosis by the radiologists. And my intestine did not grow back on its own. Once we reach adulthood our small intestine stops growing. Yet there is irrefutable medical evidence of the miracle: radiology images and reports showing the "before" and "after" lengths.

What About You?

Bruce has documented his entire story in a book titled *Saved by Angels*. This book not only chronicles his story, but deals with the most important thing in life next to being born from above: learning to hear God's voice so that we can be obedient to Him and fulfill our destiny in life…

…the spiritual gifts that have been operating in Bruce's life since he was five years old are transferable.

Everyone who knows the Messiah has these gifts. If you know Him, you too can operate in His gifts. The key is *relationship*. That is the heart of the message Bruce wants people to understand as he now travels around the world preaching and praying for people as founder of Sweet Bread Ministries. The most important thing in life is for people to have not religion, but a *relationship* with Jesus. And there is a big difference. A relationship with Jesus comes through the new birth: confessing and repenting of your sins and placing your faith in Yeshua as your Messiah—your Savior and Lord—trusting in His death as payment for your sins and in His resurrection as giving you eternal life.

Second to the new birth in Yeshua is the importance of learning how to hear God. God speaks to all of us, but so often we miss hearing because we don't know how to listen. Bruce describes hearing from God as a "word of knowledge." He explains with an example he uses in his book.

It's kind of like that old cartoon, we have this little red guy on one shoulder and an angel on the other. In the middle is us. The Bible tells us that is spiritual life. We have both angels and demons all around us. A word of knowledge is listening to the right voice. It's listening to the Holy Spirit speak inside you. When I receive a word of knowledge while ministering to people, I get excited because I know that some kind of miracle is about to happen! If the Lord tells me that someone with a bad shoulder is about to be healed and I call that person out, I know they are going to be healed!

God speaks and His miracles prove it! This principle works the same in our daily life also.

Another truth Bruce wants you to understand is how much God loves you. And knowing that God loves you should lead you to live a life pleasing to Him; a life that reflects His love. He uses as an example a dream he had repeatedly—perhaps 300 times or more over a ten-year period—in which his wife was being unfaithful to him. The dreams seemed very real. This puzzled Bruce because he knew his wife *was* faithful. When God finally explained the dream to him, Bruce understood that the dream was not about his wife, but about himself. As he relates:

> When I awoke, after having this dream the very last time, my wife was lying next to me in bed sound asleep and I kept repeating to her, "Why don't you understand how much I love you?" In fact, that was the last thing I said to her in my dream. Then I heard the Lord speaking to me and saying the same thing: "Why don't you understand how much I love you?"
>
> "I don't understand," I said. "What do you mean Lord?"
>
> "Bruce," He answered, "every time you do drugs, drink, go after money, motorcycle racing—anything you *do* to try to get peace, joy, and security, and to fill the hole that's in your heart—you are cheating on Me. Not only are you cheating on Me, but you're doing it in full sight of Me."

I knew what He meant, because ever since I was little…

…ever since that night Jesus hugged me, God has been as real to me as my hands.

I understood that every time I sought out peace through things other than God, I was being unfaithful to Him. It took me a long time to realize how I was walking with one foot in the world and one foot in God's kingdom. He wanted me to walk with both feet in His kingdom.

No matter what you have done, God still loves you. He is so good. Let me encourage you to stop the drugs and alcohol. Stop the pornography. Stop the adultery. Stop anything that you are doing to try to fill the void in your heart. Let God fill it for you. Fill it with Jesus. Anything else is a cheap substitute that can't fulfill our deepest needs! Jesus is real. He loves you, and He is calling you. He wants to hug you. Let Him surround you with His loving embrace.

Prayer of Impartation

Bruce's miraculous life began when he exercised his faith at five years old and asked Jesus to come and hug him. Jesus came and touched Bruce in such a real and tangible way that healed him emotionally and empowered him with spiritual gifts.

The Holy Spirit can do that for you today. Right now, ask the Lord to come and hug you. His presence will envelop you like liquid love. After Bruce was hugged by Jesus as a child, He was more real to Bruce than earthly realties.

Holy Spirit, I pray that you would hug this reader right now with your healing presence. I ask, God, that your liquid love would flow into every crevice of their heart and heal every emotional wound. I ask that the balm of Gilead would be applied to each wound and that full and complete restoration would take place (see Jer. 8:22).

I pray that your spiritual eyes would open, and that you would have open visions and prophetic dreams of Heaven like Bruce did.

I release over you an increasing anointing to hear God speak through words of knowledge. I pray that you would always hear the tiny whispers of God and be gently guided by His presence through even the greatest storms of your life. I pray that your relationship with Jesus would grow and deepen and that you would always be protected from "religious thinking."

I declare that the words of knowledge you deliver will touch people so deeply that it will be like they have met with Jesus face-to-face. Your words will be like honeycomb, sweet to the soul and healing to the bones (see Prov. 16:24).

I declare that when you receive words of knowledge, the miracles will be ready for you to walk in (see Eph. 2:10). Your wise words will bring healing to people (see Prov. 12:18).

I pray that your natural and spiritual children will have an encounter like Bruce did when he was five. I pray that at a young age they would feel the tangible presence of God envelop them and that it would mark them for the rest of their lives. I pray that the spiritual gifts that you will walk in in your lifetime will transfer to them, and that they will walk in an even greater measure than you will.

I pray that the Word of God would sow great faith into their hearts at a young age and would guide them for the rest of their lives (see Prov. 22:6).

As a child of God who seeks your face, you will be filled with the Holy Spirit and equipped to draw others to God. You will be a person of great understanding who draws a person out and ministers to them (see Prov. 20:5). Amen.

For more information about Bruce's ministry, please visit his Website at www.sweetbreadministries.com.

Chapter Five

SUPERNATURAL SURGERY

Human surgeons perform natural surgery every day, but have you ever heard of *supernatural* surgery? That is what Jennifer Toledo experienced in a hospital in Kenya after she contracted a rare and deadly disease. With no cure, the doctors saw no recourse but to operate on her dying organs in the hope of helping her recover. It wasn't necessary. In a dream Jennifer saw Jesus enter her hospital room, open her up with His hand, massage each of her organs, then close her up again. She was completely healed.

Jennifer is no stranger to supernatural encounters. When she was seven, and in the absence of her earthly father, God told her that He would be her "Daddy." Years later, as a young adult, Jennifer had a vision of Heaven where she saw Jesus weeping over all the injustices of the world. There she received an impartation of His heart of compassion, especially for children, and it changed her forever. Let's listen to her story.

When I was seven my dad left home. How well I remember that day! I was devastated. I was in my room crying and praying and asking the Lord, "Who's going to take care of me? Who's going to be my daddy?" In one of the clearest instances I have ever had of hearing God's voice, He spoke to me very sweetly and said, "I'll be your Daddy." It was very simple but it was all my little seven-year old heart needed to hear. From that day to this God has continued to prove Himself as my Father.

Growing up in a single parent household, we didn't have a lot of money, but we learned how faithfully God answers prayer. There were many times where we literally had to trust Him to provide even the simplest things, like food, that earthly fathers normally provide for their children. On days when there was no food in the house we would pray, "God, You're our Dad, and dads feed their kids. We need food." It was a simple prayer, but one that we prayed with absolute faith. I remember many times going to school with no food in the house and walking home in the afternoon to find bags of groceries left on our doorstep. Then we would celebrate and rejoice at how God had miraculously provided. No one ever left a note, so we never knew where the food came from, but this kind of thing happened all throughout my childhood.

A Critical Choice

Even though Jennifer witnessed countless instances of God's miraculous provision when she was growing up, by the time she entered her teen years, like so many other young people, she felt the world pulling her in a different direction. She tried unsuccessfully to walk with a foot in both worlds until one day when she was 16 and heard her Daddy's voice again. She recalls:

> At that time I really loved God but was still very selfish. One day as I was sitting in Taco Bell with some friends I suddenly began to sense the conviction of the Holy Spirit. God was tugging at my heart and I heard Him say to me very clearly, "You need to make a decision. You can't keep living this way. Either you are going to live for me or you are going to live for yourself, but you cannot do both." That really struck me because I thought I *could* do both. At that moment I realized for the first time a little of what it means to die to yourself and live for God. I began a process of surrender that day that has become the journey of my whole life since then.

The Weeping Room

The more Jennifer walked the path of surrender, the more she desired to know the heart of God. That is a "dangerous" pursuit because whenever God reveals Himself, nothing is ever the same again. Jennifer experienced this first hand when in a vision God took her to Heaven. What she saw there altered the course of her life forever. She continues her story:

> My heart's desire was to know what was precious to God's heart. One day as I was seeking this, I had a

vision in which Jesus took me up to Heaven. I saw what I can only explain as the Father's house. It had many rooms and each room contained many different things. He took me into one room called the "intimacy chamber." From there He led me to another room. From the doorway I could see that it was a very simple, very humble room with a little wooden chair and a window.

As I began to enter the room He said to me, "Think about it before you go in, because this is a lonely place." I wondered why there would be a place like that in heaven; it didn't make sense to me. Then He said, "This is where I spend most of My time."

"What's the name of this room?" I asked.

He replied, "It is the 'weeping room'."

I didn't understand what He meant until He sat on the chair and looked out the window...

In that place He began to share His heart with me about the poor, the broken, the children, and issues of injustice in the world.

From that window He could see every single cry coming from the earth at one time; every person crying out; every prayer; every act of injustice; He saw it all. He heard everything. As I watched Him sitting there taking it all in I began to weep. I was overwhelmed by the beauty of a God who would choose to see the pain, the suffering, and the cares of mankind and listen to all the cries of hurting people.

This is so true of the Lord. Speaking prophetically of Messiah Yeshua, Isaiah said, *"In all their affliction He was afflicted"* (Isa. 63:9a NKJV). Imagine that: the Creator of the universe declaring that He is afflicted in our afflictions. He feels our pain and knows our sorrows. What a great God! What compassion! And it was in witnessing this compassion of Jesus in the weeping room, how He wept over the suffering of children and over all the injustices throughout the world, where God sealed compassion in Jennifer's heart. As she recalls:

> When I was in the weeping room I began to see all of the things that move the heart of God. For the first time I began to feel His emotions. It is one thing to know in your head that God is compassionate, yet quite another to actually feel what He feels. That's the kind of person I wanted to be, so I asked the Lord to brand compassion on my heart. I knew it would cost me a lot, because compassion will drive you to lay your life down. But He did it. In my vision He took a branding iron and branded the word "Compassion" on my heart. My continuing prayer has been that God would use me as a vessel of His compassion. My experience in the weeping room totally changed the course of my life.

Lightning on Goat Mountain

Jennifer says that children are by far the group most victimized by injustice throughout the world today. Out of a total global population of 6.5 billion, 2.2 billion are under the age of 15. Sadly, half of all children (at least 1 billion) live in dire poverty where disease and starvation are daily realities. In some parts of the world many children are forced into prostitution or sold into sexual slavery. Others are forced to become soldiers and calloused killers by warlords desperate for fighters. Jennifer's compassionate heart has placed her at the forefront of ministry to rescue the world's children from poverty, starvation, abuse, and exploitation. During one such trip to Africa she encountered deeply entrenched demonic evil and witnessed the overcoming power of God. It was a showdown reminiscent of Elijah and the prophets of Baal on Mount Carmel (see 1 Kings 18:17-40). Jennifer describes what happened.

It was my first trip into Africa. I was 21 and really didn't know what I was getting into. We ran into trouble from the beginning. First, we arrived in Africa only to discover that we had no money. The assistance we had counted on had been cut off. Second, I learned very quickly that many parts of Africa discriminate against women. I went into one of the most difficult places in northern Kenya, called the Turkana. The whole environment was extremely hostile, very difficult on every level. The tribe I was working with was, in fact, in a blood covenant with satan, and had been for several generations. They had to offer all sorts of blood sacrifices to appease the devil; otherwise, horrible things would happen to them. Their huts would catch fire. Family members would bleed from the nose until they died. These poor people lived continually in terrible fear yet continued to pay homage to the demons because they didn't know how to escape. Their whole land was under the curse as well.

On the surface, the situation appeared hopeless. No one in the village would turn to Jesus because if they did they would have the witch doctors after them. At first all I could do was pray because the circumstances were so overwhelming. Poverty, famine, drought, war, and violence were on every side. At one point I called out to God and said, "Lord, why am I here? What's this all about?"

In response God asked me a very simple question. He said, "Jennifer, do you believe that I still use Davids to take down Goliaths?"

I had to think about that for a minute. Finally I said, "Of course I believe that. You are the God of miracles and I know you can do it." Yet inside I was thinking, "Surely You can't mean me, and surely You can't mean this place." Nevertheless I began to ask God for a simple strategy, and to show me His heart for that place and those people. After my encounter with compassion in the weeping room, my heart was so moved for those people and I really wanted to see spiritual transformation come to that place.

When we asked God for a strategy He told us to draw all the leaders of the region together since it was the leaders who originally put the tribe in the curse. All the leaders came together, and for seven days hundreds of pastors, tribal leaders, and government leaders repented of their covenants with the enemy and broke the curses on themselves, their people, and the land. Then God revealed to us that the only way they could come out of covenant with satan was to enter into a stronger blood covenant. So the *whole tribe* corporately came into blood covenant with Jesus the Messiah. It was absolutely amazing.

And as for the witch doctors?

When the whole tribe entered into blood covenant with Jesus, God showed up instantly in power. There was a complete shift in the atmosphere and we asked God for miraculous signs.

It had not rained there in years and people were dying because of the drought. Suddenly, rain began to pour down right in the middle of the desert. A huge bolt of lightning struck a nearby mountain called Goat

Mountain, which was the high place for the witch doctors, the seat of their demonic power. They came running down the mountain in fear because their power had dried up. Something had changed. God stepped in, the curse was broken, and many of those witch doctors ended up getting delivered, saved, and set free.

Divine Surgery

Whenever satan suffers a major defeat it is only a matter of time before he launches a counterattack. After the miracle at Goat Mountain, the enemy set his sights on Jennifer. She contracted a rare and deadly tropical disease and almost died. Humanly speaking, there was no hope. But Jennifer was in the hands of the God who was her Daddy and had taken care of her since she was seven. Another miracle was in store.

> I got very sick and didn't know what was happening. But I knew I was in very bad shape. They rushed me to a hospital that was 14 hours away, and even getting there was a miracle. Once there, I was told that had I arrived only a few hours later I would have been dead. All of my organs had begun to shut down. The toxin in my body was completely destroying everything inside me. The doctors told me there really wasn't much they could do. Although they did not hold out much hope, they wanted to try surgery in an effort to salvage whatever they could.

Something rose up inside of me and I said,...

**No. I'm not going to have this
surgery. I know that Jesus
can heal me. He is my Dad.**

I said, "Since I was seven years old He has taken care of
me and has provided for me. He will not fail me now."
I began to stand on the promises in the Bible. Later, as
I was praying in bed, I fell asleep and in a dream saw
Jesus walk into my hospital room. He took the back of
His hand, cut me open like a surgeon, and pulled my
skin back. It didn't hurt at all. Then one by one He began to massage my organs, and put them back in. He
cleaned some things out and then He smiled and said,
"It's good." After that He closed my skin back up. He
had my perfect color skin in His hand and put it back
on top. In my dream I was celebrating because I would
not have a scar.

Right after this I awakened from my dream and, quite
honestly, I still felt ill. But I had to make a choice. I
asked myself, "What is the nature of God? Would
He give me this dream to tease me? I don't think He

would." So I began to declare, "I'm healed; I'm healed," even though I was in pain. But every time I said, "I'm healed," supernatural strength came into my body. I kept getting stronger and stronger. All in all I was extremely ill for ten days in very poor condition and didn't eat anything during that time. Then, on that last day, I was completely and totally healed, and without surgery. Jesus performed my surgery.

Naturally, of course, the doctors could not believe me at first. They came running in and rushed me off for testing. I had multiple tests and every single test came back exactly the same: no disease. These were the same doctors that had tested me initially. "This is medically undefined," they admitted. "We can't explain it. This morning her organs weren't functioning; now all of her organs are functioning 100 percent, and there is no poison in her body. She is completely healed. We have no explanation."

A Father Who Loves You

Everybody needs a father. No matter who you are, young or old, man or woman, boy or girl, you need a father in your life who loves you. Maybe your earthly father, like mine, is dead. Perhaps you never knew your father or, as in Jennifer's case, he may have left when you were young. Whatever your situation, whether your earthly father is with you or not, Jennifer wants you to know that you have a heavenly Father who loves you more than you can possibly imagine. He says to all of us, *"I have loved you with an everlasting love; Therefore with lovingkindness I have drawn you"* (Jer. 31:3b).

Children are totally dependent on their parents. In the same way we as children of God are totally dependent on Him. Yet many Christians forget what it is like to be a child. They have forgotten their first love. They have forgotten that God wants to be their Daddy. As long as you insist on being self-sufficient, you will never fully experience the fatherly love of God. He wants you to. He wants to be your Daddy. Will you let Him?

How important is it to know that God the Father is your Daddy? Here is Jennifer's answer:

It's everything! I just want you to know that no matter who you are, no matter what you are going through, no matter what is happening in your life, God is faithful. If you give Him a chance, He will prove Himself to you as a faithful, loving Father. I can't imagine going through my life without knowing the love of my Father. Nothing escapes His loving, compassionate eye. He sees every act of injustice. He sees the wrongs that have been done. He sees the circumstances in your life—and He cares. Surrender your life to Him. Let Him be your Daddy. He will prove Himself faithful. Your Daddy will turn your circumstances around.

The next move is yours. God has already made His move. He says to all of us, "I love you," and proved it at the cross. Can you comprehend this?

The Creator of the universe reached down in the form of a man named Jesus to pay the price for your sins and to heal your diseases.

Your sins have separated you from the greatest love in the universe, the love that you've been looking for your whole life. Don't turn away from Him because of fear or shame. He will not reject you. God is real, and God is love. How do you respond to that kind of love? Repent of your sins. Turn away from your sins in faith and in faith turn to Jesus. Trust in His death as payment for your sins and acknowledge Him as Savior and Lord of your life. Rely on Him. Start calling out, "Daddy I need you." That's called being a child, and that's what Jennifer is talking about. We must become like little children. God wants to be your Daddy. Will you come to Him as His child?

Prayer of Impartation

Jennifer's story is amazing, as God taught her from a young age that He is our Father and our provider. Jennifer allowed the miracles of provision she witnessed as a child to change the way that she *expected* God to interact with her. She knew God would heal her because He had always provided for her and she had seen Him heal others.

Would you like to interact with God in a way that *expects* God to answer? Would you like to hear divine direction, perform miracles, and see signs confirm that God is working in our midst?

I'm going to pray that this same realm of child-like faith would be opened up to you.

In the name of Jesus, I pray that you would receive a revelation that God is your Father and provider. I pray that this revelation would completely transform the way you *expect* God to interact with you. I pray that you would gain such a confidence that God is working with you that it empowers you to step out in great boldness and see mighty miracles.

I release over you the ability to allow small miracles to build faith for larger miracles. I pray that, like Jennifer, you would defeat your own Goliaths and walk out your own Bible story. I pray that you would inspire others to believe that God would use them as Davids to defeat Goliaths for the glory of God.

I pray that your ability to hear God's voice would increase and equip you to walk out the calling God has on your life. I pray for divine strategies to defeat the enemy and his strongholds. I ask, Father, that these strategies would be confirmed with signs and wonders so that all would know you are doing a mighty work in the land.

Jennifer's Bible-story lifestyle began when she started to ask God what was precious to His heart. She was invited into a spiritual encounter that gave her access to God's most intimate concerns. You too can have access to God's heart if you seek Him.

I pray for a spirit of faithfulness to rest on everyone reading this book so that they would walk in consistent relationship with God, grow in intimacy with Him, and would earn spiritual promotions and Kingdom authority. Amen.

To find out more about Jennifer's ministry, please visit www.gcmovement.org.

Chapter Six

FROM HELL TO HEAVEN

When Earthquake Kelley was a professional boxer, no one knew the hidden truth about the battles he fought throughout his life against the demonic forces bent on his destruction. Beaten and abused daily by his father, he was taking drugs at the age of four. At the age of five he began dabbling in voodoo and went on to become a voodoo priest and a master of witchcraft. As he got older, his powers increased to the point where he could cast spells and kill people by cursing them and even leave his own body at will. He soon died from a drug overdose and went to hell. God literally lifted him out of hell and brought him back to life. Not long after this, he was radically saved in a Pentecostal church and gave his life completely to God.

Some years later, Earthquake died a second time from a brain aneurysm. He found himself transported to Heaven, where he saw his murdered son, as well as many other children who had died from war, violence, neglect, abuse, and abortion, and where he was given a message from God to deliver to the world. As you read his story you will be sobered by the reality of hell, comforted by the reality of Heaven, and encouraged by the amazing power of God that can bring people back from the dead.

A descendant (on his father's side) from slaves owned by an Irish plantation owner named John Kelley, "Earthquake" Kelley earned his unusual nickname with his prowess in the boxing ring. After he knocked down an opponent with a single punch during a 1983 elimination bout for the 1984 Los Angeles Olympics, a sports announcer at the time said of him, "That guy hits like an earthquake," and the name stuck. "Earthquake" himself believes God gave him that name even earlier, when in a vision he heard God say, "Because of you the ground is shaking; because of you the ground is broken." It was a prophetic statement related to the impact he would have for the kingdom of God.

Earthquake also inherited something else from his father's family line: a legacy of voodoo and witchcraft. Beginning at age five, he was a fourth-generation practitioner of these occult "arts," which dominated his life until Jesus set him free as a teenager. Along the way he had several close brushes with death from demonic spirits that sought to destroy him. It started even before he was born. As he explains:

Despite his voodoo heritage, my father married a Pentecostal Christian.

So from the very beginning there was a "tug-of-war" on my life.

My mother told me after I was grown that my father didn't even want me to be born. He even forced her to get an abortion. She said that at the abortion clinic they used needles to try to kill me in the womb, but that she was supernaturally protected. During the procedure, she felt another hand inside her shielding me from the needles.

When the abortion failed, my father took matters into his own hands. He beat my mother severely and did other awful things to her trying to destroy me on the inside. But still God said, "No." He had a purpose for me and I survived by the grace of God.

Voodoo Master

Even after Earthquake was born his father didn't let up, and he beat him almost every day. There were other negative factors at work to the point that it seems a miracle that he survived childhood. At four he started taking drugs. At five he entered the world that would dominate his childhood and early teen years and which almost destroyed him: voodoo. It began with his grandmother. He describes what happened.

One day when I was five I saw my grandmother use voodoo against someone. The man keeled over right then and there. I was shocked, impressed, and interested all at the same moment. After all, there was a lot of power at work for somebody to say a few words and make a grown man fall over backwards. My response was like, "Wow! I want some of that."

So I tried it. I spoke the same words I heard my grandmother say, and as soon as I said them it felt like something started swirling around and got on the inside of me. I became possessed, and that started a downhill spiral in my life.

As he grew older, Earthquake sank deeper and deeper into the realm of voodoo and witchcraft. The drug use continued—along with drug dealing—and by the age of 13 he was even involved in pimping and prostitution. His life began to take a decisive turn, however, the day his father brought home a witch to mentor him and prepare him for the next level in his rise to become an occult master. But they were about to see the awesome power of God and of a mother's prayers.

The witch told me that because of my Haitian background I was to be sent to Haiti to work under "Papa Doc" Duvalier; to be raised up under the president of the country to control the people through voodoo. In voodoo they deal with numbers just as Christians do, but they counterfeit everything God has. Seven is an important number in voodoo, and they picked me to go to Port au Prince because I was the seventh child in my family.

At the time I was floored at the idea because I was really into the "power" thing and really wanted to go. I had already seen some powerful things happen through voodoo and I wanted more of that power. So when the witch told me that I could have free reign down in Haiti, I was all for it: the power, the money, the control, being a child over a lot of grownups. Things like that excited me, so I was ready to go. I would have gone, too, except for my mother. Thank God, I had a praying mother, or who knows what would have happened to me!

One day when my dad, the witch, and I were together, the witch packed a little brown suitcase for me and said to me, "This is the day for you. I am going to take you into Manhattan and put you on a boat to Port au Prince." Their plan was to sneak me out the back door, put me in a car, and take me to the ship. As we were trying to creep out the back door, my mother came out of nowhere. "Where are you taking my baby?" she challenged. The witch said, "He is no longer your child; he belongs to me." My mother shouted, "No way!" and began pulling me by the arm. The witch pulled me by my other arm and I was jerked back and forth like a tug-of-war.

Finally, my father and the witch got me away from my mother and pushed me toward the back door. Before they could get me outside, however, something unusual happened. They both saw something so big and so awesome that it scared them to the point where they suddenly let me go and ran out the door. I don't know for sure what they saw, but I know my mother was praying and I believe God must have sent an angel to prevent them from taking me down to Port au Prince.

Even though Earthquake never went to Haiti, he remained deeply immersed in voodoo and witchcraft. The witch gave him the names of dozens of demons and taught him how to summon them and send them to inflict harm on specific people. He also learned how to astral project—the occult practice of willingly leaving his body. It seemed he was destined for greatness as a voodoo master...until he encountered a power greater than his own.

> At that particular time I had a couple of friends who became believers in Jesus. I didn't like it because I thought they had abandoned me, so I sent a couple of evil spirits after them and said, "Curse them. I want you to destroy everything they are doing." Those spirits came back to me and said, "We couldn't touch them." I said, "I command you to go back and put a curse on them." They returned a second time and said, "We can't touch them; they are protected." So I astral projected out of my own body and went to see for myself. When I got there I saw my two friends surrounded by eight-foot-tall angels with swords that protected them everywhere they went. I recognized immediately why the spirits I sent couldn't do anything. My friends had access to power that was much stronger than anything I had; they were protected by giant angels.

To Hell and Back

Earthquake's friends may have had angels to protect them, but he was about to discover that the demonic forces that gave him his power were actually out to destroy him. A drug overdose stopped his heart. Once again, it was the prayers of his mother that saved him and brought him back literally from the brink of hell.

I had just turned fifteen and a voice inside said, "You have never really been high. Why don't you go for a really super high so you can brag to all your friends in the drug community about how you can hold your dope?" Then the voice told me what I needed to do. I had some pills that were so strong that ¼ of one pill would keep you high for eight days. So to start with, I took three or four of those. Then I smoked some weed, did about five or six hundred dollars worth of cocaine all at once, and drank some beer. I hated beer but I was in a bar and the bartender told me I had to drink or go home. He knew I was underage and still gave me the beer on top of everything else I had taken. It was too much for me. I passed out.

My buddies who were with me put me in the car to take me home. On the way home I died. The overdose with its overpowering combination of drugs stopped my heart. Immediately, evil spirits appeared, snatched me out of my body, pulled me down into a pit and started tormenting me. They were coming from everywhere. They were in my mouth, they were in my eyes, they were hitting me with all kinds of things. They were yelling and telling me that I worked for them, that it was all a trap, a setup. "You did all our bidding for us," they screamed, "and now you are in hell." It was horrible...

...I discovered right then that hell is real. It was not made for us.

Hell was designed for the devil and his fallen angels, but that's where I was.

That overdose was a setup from the pits of hell. The drugs were a trick to stop my heart and get me lost for eternity. Hell is a lonely, miserable, ugly, stinking, sulfur-smelling, nasty, pitiful, horrible place, and that doesn't even begin to describe it. I saw all kinds of horror and misery. All around me people were screaming in torment and I was right there among them.

All of a sudden, hands of light came down inside that pit, grabbed me by my shoulders and started to pull me out. The whole time the evil spirits tried to hold onto me saying, "He's ours! He belongs to us!" But those hands of light pulled me out of there and put me back in my own body. Then I heard a voice say, "Because of your mother's prayers, you have been spared for the work you have been chosen to do."

When I heard the voice, I said, "Oh God, I've been to hell!" I was so wicked and messed up that at that point I didn't even know to thank God for saving me. I just knew something extraordinary had happened.

Saved to Serve

Earthquake managed to make it home. He had survived a drug overdose that by any account should have killed him. The only reason he did survive was by the grace of God. But even this close call was not enough to convince Earthquake to change his ways. By his own admission, he was so "messed up" that even after the wake-up call of a visit to hell, he continued to deal drugs. He continued his godless lifestyle. In fact, he was getting ready to cash in on a huge drug deal. But God had other plans.

The turning point for Earthquake began when one of his sisters invited him to church. As he explains:

My sister kept telling me, "You need to be saved." My trip to hell should have gotten through to me, but at that time there was a big shipment of drugs coming in and my cut was a million dollars. For a 15-year-old kid a million dollars was a big thing. I didn't want to go to church, but my sister insisted, so I went.

When we got there I said to her, "Sit me in the back." I was mad and didn't want to be around Pentecostal anything.

So she sat me in the back. The preacher preached, and when it was over I said, "Okay, good. I'm finished."

The next night my sister said, "You're going back."

I said, "No, I'm not going back to church anymore. I'm finished with church. I've got to get out of here. I have a drug deal, the biggest one we've ever had."

She was adamant. "No, you're going to church."

Finally I said, "Okay, I'll go to church." This went on for two or three days. One night when I was sitting in church the preacher suddenly called out, "Hey you in the back; young man." I didn't know he was talking to me; I thought he was talking to somebody else. Everybody in the church turned around to see who he was talking to, so I turned around too. I was the only one in the back, so then I knew he meant me. He said, "Come up here in the front. God wants to save you."

I got mad. I said to myself, "I don't want all this Jesus stuff; I've got things to do...."

**...But then I heard a voice
inside me say, "I love you."**

The voice said, "Remember when they had a gun to your head and it wouldn't go off, but instead went up in the air? That was Me." He reminded me of all the times He had spared me when a drug deal went bad or when I was almost killed or this that and the other. Finally, He said, "Go up there. I want to save you and use you."

After that I couldn't help myself. I got out of that seat and went to the front. The pastor told me everything I had been involved in. It was like he had been right there with me as I was growing up. He just read everything off to me, how I was in voodoo and witchcraft and how I put curses on people; somehow he knew everything.

"How can you know all of that?" I asked him. "You don't even know me." But it was God that told him. At the same time God was speaking to me and saying, "I will use you. I can do more for you than anyone else can."

I said, "Hold it, God. You know what I do. I am a wicked person. I do bad things to people. I put curses on them and they die." But thanks be to God, His love overcame my objections, and He saved me. I gave my heart to Jesus. It was like a ton of bricks fell off of me. He has been using me ever since.

A Tragic Loss

Earthquake's life was transformed when he gave his heart to Jesus. He began preaching the gospel of salvation and deliverance in Messiah Jesus. He and his wife Selena opened their home to street people, the homeless, drug addicts, homosexuals, and others who had no one to care for them. Between 1981 and 2001, they took in at least 50 people and showed and taught them the love of Jesus. They also raised a family, including three sons. Life was good, and they were happy. Then came a premonition of tragedy. Earthquake relates what happened:

> On December 6, 1998, my son Scott and I were in the kitchen sparring a little bit. I had three sons, and as an ex-professional boxer I wanted to make them tough, so I taught them the moves and we used play around and hit at each other. They usually couldn't hit me. I would dart and dance around and say, "Your old man is pretty smooth, huh." On this particular day Scott still couldn't hit me, but he suddenly stopped in the middle of things, grabbed me and clutched me close to him. That's when I realized he was crying.
>
> I said, "Hey man, what's the matter? What's wrong?" I felt bad because I thought I may have hit him too hard.
>
> "No Dad," he said, "you didn't hit me too hard." Then through his tears he said, "Dad, I want you to promise me that you will never stop preaching deliverance and you will never stop helping the least, the last and the lost people who are coming through here. Promise me that you'll never stop ministering to people."
>
> "I promise," I told him. "I will continue to do that."
>
> Scott then let go of me and ran out of the house crying.

"What happened?" my wife asked. "What's wrong?"

"I don't know," I answered. "He just told me not to stop preaching and helping people."

The next day I was in Nevada preaching a message when my wife called me. I could tell by the sound of her voice that something was wrong. She told me that Scott had been car-jacked and that the thieves had shot him at point-blank range. He was dead.

Scott somehow had a premonition that something bad was going to happen to him. It was like he was getting ready to go home to be with the Lord.

Ascent to Heaven

Earthquake had trouble recovering from Scott's death, and his life started going downhill. He was still casting demons out of people, but then the demons starting causing people to come after him, so he was under a lot of spiritual attack. He says he was not backslidden so much as in rebellion.

I was rebelling against God because I had asked Him to remove some of the pressure I was under from other people. It seemed to me that God was taking His own sweet time and I wanted Him to hurry up. So I started telling God that unless He took away the pressure I would pull back from the deliverance messages that I was preaching and start preaching those good old "seeker-sensitive" "Golden Rule" messages.

Before long I developed a very bad headache. At first I didn't think much of it. Being an ex-boxer, I just thought one of my old fights was catching up to me. After two days my wife convinced me to go to the hospital, where they discovered that I had a brain aneurysm. I had no idea. I was like a dead man walking. Not long after this, I suffered a massive brain hemorrhage.

Earthquake actually died on the operating table. This time, instead of descending into hell, he left his body and ascended to Heaven. He describes what he saw...

...when I was in Paradise, I saw an angel about seven or eight feet tall with wings covered with gold flakes.

He told me to walk around. As far as I could see, everything was absolutely beautiful. There were flowers like I had never seen before, and well-manicured grass with a diamond or emerald in each blade. The colors were like nothing we see on earth.

I walked along a river that looked like liquid diamonds and issued forth from a big, beautiful golden palace.

Then I heard the voices of what must have been angels singing, far better than any choir I ever heard on earth. It looked as though everything was working together: the grass swaying, the river moving, the angels singing. Huge trees were all around and they looked like they were bowing down and praising God. There were no shadows anywhere. Nothing in Heaven casts a shadow because the light hits from all over. It is just a beautiful, radiant, awesome place.

As I walked along the edge of the river, I saw someone on the other side and he saw me. It was my son Scott. I called out to him, "Scott, it's you, it's you! How do I get over to that side where you are?" I wanted to get over there just to give him a hug.

But Scott said, "You can't come in here now, Dad. You have to go back. You made God a promise, and you made me a promise that you would finish the work that you have to do."

"No," I said, "I don't want to go back. I want to stay here in this place with you." I started looking for a boat, a tire, a raft—anything to get over there. I didn't want to come back here because Heaven was so awesome. My headache was gone. There was no pain whatsoever. I could feel the presence of God everywhere. Everywhere I stepped it felt as though God was embracing me with His love.

Children in Heaven

Earthquake did not want to leave Heaven but finally accepted the fact that it was not time for him to stay. But before he left, he was shown one more thing that related to the message the Lord gave him to share with the world when he returned: the children of Heaven.

As I felt myself being pulled away from my son by what felt like an invisible hand, I saw three groups of children running and playing and having fun. They seemed to be having such a great time that I wanted to join them. That's when I heard God's voice. "You are wondering who those children are, aren't you?"

"Yes," I replied. "Who are they?"

He said, "The first group of children you see are those who were murdered, or killed in wars, or left for dead. They are with Me now."

He showed me the second group. "Do you see these children?" He asked. "I had a purpose for them, something special in My heart for them to do for me through the Kingdom. They were going to change a lot of things on the earth for good. But because of the sickness and hardness of men and of women, they were aborted and sent back."

That's when His voice started changing, as if He was hurt through His heart; trembling as though He was starting to cry. I was amazed. I had no idea that the Lord had that kind of emotion. But He did. He hurt deeply over the condition of these abortions. It looked like tears were about to drop out of His eyes and I felt as though if one of those tears came out it would be as big as an Olympic-sized swimming pool. I couldn't deal with it. I said, "Lord I didn't know you hurt like this."

He showed me the third group. "Do you see that group over there running and playing?" He asked.

"Yes Lord," I replied. "Who are they?"

And He said, "They are the children I sent to so-called church people, to so-called Christian homes; people who did not trust me, who believed in the ways of the world, who did not believe that I would take care of them and another mouth to feed. So instead of trusting Me, they aborted the child I sent them."

What About You?

Drawing from the experiences of his own life and especially his vision of Heaven, Earthquake has a couple of messages he wants people to hear. The first has to do with the sanctity of life and is directed at those men and women who find themselves faced with an unexpected or undesired pregnancy. Under such circumstances, it is easy to feel overwhelmed by fear and uncertainty. Earthquake encourages you, in the midst of the clamor of competing voices, to listen to the only voice that matters: the voice of God.

Maybe you feel like God has abandoned you, or put you down, and you feel defeated and ready to give up. Many voices clamor for your attention and you are not sure which voice to listen to. I know something about voices, and trust me, there is only one voice you need to listen to and that's the voice of God. Life is precious and sacred. Do not destroy that life inside you, that life you have created, because no matter your circumstances, God has allowed that life to be in you so that you can nurture that life in the things of God so that this little person can grow up to be a great man or woman of God. Choose life.

The second message Earthquake wants to leave with you has to do with forgiveness, particularly forgiveness toward God for His perceived mistreatment of you. An unforgiving spirit will always hold you back, so Earthquake says to let it go.

There are many people today, even Christians, who are holding things against God because He didn't give them what they wanted when they wanted it. Somebody they prayed for died, or they lost a job, or went through a divorce, or a child was murdered, or they lost their house through a fire, flood, earthquake or some other "act of God" natural disaster...

...when bad things happen it is easy to blame God even though it is not His fault.

God is not to blame for the hardship and problems in the world; it is the sinfulness of man that is responsible. God loves you and wants to make all things new in your life but He cannot until you get rid of your unforgiving spirit toward Him or anyone else. Until you forgive Him, who has never sinned, He will not be able to forgive you and move you on to the things that He has for you to do.

Prayer of Impartation

Earthquake's testimony is so powerful and reminds us that Jesus is more powerful than any other god that people worship.

After Earthquake surrendered his life to Jesus, he has seen many miracles including deliverance from demonic possession. Signs and wonders follow his ministry.

God is calling all of us into a deeper level of intimacy and holiness with Himself. Earthquake encourages us to stop blaming God for the bad things that happen in life and to forgive others for their mistreatment of us. God is not capable of sin, and He has not sinned against us. If there's someone that you need to forgive, release that to God right now.

Father, I ask forgiveness for blaming You for the bad things that have happened to me in life. I accept the truth that You love me and are always for me, not against me.

In the name of Jesus, I forgive every person who has hurt me. I ask for Your strength to stop punishing them for their sin, since You have already paid for all sin with Your life. I release them from all condemnation and guilt. Amen.

After renouncing voodoo and turning to Jesus, Earthquake Kelley gained great spiritual authority over demonic powers. He now has a ministry to those influenced by demonic powers. Think about your own testimony, about the things that God has delivered you from. You have authority over the things that Jesus has delivered you from.

I pray that God would remind you of the victories you have gained through your relationship with Him. I declare that your personal testimony will inspire others to trust Jesus for their salvation and deliverance. Your words will set the captives free.

I pray that your own awareness of the spiritual authority you carry as a believer will grow. I speak to the incomparably great power that dwells in you because of the Messiah's redemption and I call it to rise up in you and touch people through you (see Eph. 1:19).

You are God's workmanship, and He has prepared good works, miracles, signs, wonders, healings, and salvations for you to walk in (see Eph. 2:10). You will call the gold out in people, and they will embrace their identity as a child of God. You will build up others according to their needs, and it will benefit those who listen (see Eph. 4:29).

For further information about Earthquake's ministry, please visit www.earthquakekelleyministries.org.

Chapter Seven

SEEING THE INVISIBLE

Jonathan Welton is a young man with a rare ability: he can see clearly into the invisible world. This is not a natural ability but a supernatural gift he received through an impartation of the Holy Spirit. This gift, which the Bible calls the gift of discerning of spirits, enables Jonathan to perceive spiritual realities in the natural world that most of the rest of us cannot see. His heightened spiritual vision gives him unusual insight—"sight of knowledge" if you will—into the hurts, pain, and needs of people he comes into contact with, allowing him to become an agent of healing in their lives. Furthermore, Jonathan says that this same gift is available to every believer. Everyone who follows Messiah Yeshua has the potential to walk in greater spiritual discernment. As you read Jonathan's story you will be encouraged to believe that you, too, can learn to see the invisible.

Jonathan Welton wasn't supposed to be here. His parents already had two children, a girl and a boy, and thought they were finished with having kids. Then one day during a worship service, the Spirit of God spoke to Jonathan's mother and asked her if she wanted another child. He told her that there was someone He wanted to be born at that specific time for a specific purpose. She was free to choose whether or not to have that child, but if she chose not to, the Lord would find someone else. He was determined to have this child born at that specific time. Jonathan's mother said yes, and Jonathan was born.

So there was a foreshadowing of specific divine purpose over Jonathan's life from the very beginning. His life was pretty normal until he was 19, when one day, minding his own business, Jonathan went to a meeting where a prophet singled him out. God turned his life upside down that day. He describes what happened:

> This prophet asked me to stand up and then began to speak a word of prophecy over me. He said, "Jonathan, the Lord is going to give you the gift of discerning of spirits. He has called you as a seer." At the time I didn't even know what a "seer" was. I soon learned that a seer is a prophetic individual who operates in a high level of discerning of spirits. Then the prophet said, "You're going to start discerning spirits more than you ever wanted to." Up to that point I had *never* wanted to, so anything at all would have been impressive compared to my previous experiences....

...instantly I received an impartation through this prophetic word and began to see things in the Spirit.

The first thing I remember seeing was a bookshelf in my house that had fire on it. As I walked over to it the Lord told me that there were specific books there that I needed to read. So I began to pull them down. They were by different leaders who taught on the prophetic, and on the discerning of spirits. The Lord was guiding me into the books I needed to grow and to learn in that gift at that time.

Many people are confused about the nature of the gift of discerning of spirits. Because of this confusion, Jonathan says, this particular spiritual gift has gotten somewhat of a bad rap among believers. As Jonathan explains:

Discerning of spirits is one of the nine spiritual gifts listed in First Corinthians chapter 12, and is actually a gift that has been given a bad reputation. Many Christians associate the gift with the discerning of evil or demonic spirits, which is true, but there is much more to this gift than just discerning darkness. It also involves discerning the presence of the Holy Spirit, heavenly spirits (or angels), and the human spirit as well.

Thirty Days of Open Vision

Immediately upon receiving this impartation of the gift of discerning of spirits, Jonathan's spiritual eyes were opened and he entered a 30-day period of open vision that almost overwhelmed him because he could not understand at first what he was seeing. In his words:

After he prophesied over me, a window of time opened up where for 30 days I saw things in the Spirit all the time, and it overwhelmed me. I would walk down the street and see serpents wrapped around certain buildings, or demonic beings on top of certain buildings. I would go into a store and see objects sticking out of people: swords, spears, arrows. I started seeing angels in different places. I would go to worship services and see angels in the room, and sometimes, if the worship was cut off prematurely, such as if the speaker got up to share too soon, I would see the angels crying. These kinds of visions went on for 30 days. The whole thing was so overwhelming that I stayed home as much as I could because it was too scary to go out. All the time I kept reading those books and asking the Lord, "What is it I am encountering here?" To be honest, I was not enjoying the experience because I didn't understand what I was seeing.

Another characteristic of Jonathan's gift was that he discovered he could discern whether someone was a believer simply by looking at the person. In fact, he says, that was one of the things he saw most clearly.

I could always identify believers because they carried the glory of God. Whenever I saw them, a radiant light was shining out in all directions from behind them. In the same way, I could identify non-believers by the veil of darkness around them. Second Corinthians 4:4 says that the god of this age has veiled the eyes of the unbeliever. There is literally a veil that surrounds a nonbeliever.

Sometimes I would see a believer surrounded by a cloud of darkness that was oppressing the light shining out of them, and I learned to recognize this as an indication that this believer was being oppressed by depression or sickness.

But then, after 30 days, as quickly as the gift came, it lifted. Suddenly everything seemed to be back to normal. As frightened and overwhelmed as he had felt when the experience began, Jonathan was just as concerned when it stopped. He didn't know what had happened.

I thought maybe I had done something horrible. I said, "Lord, what exactly was that all about? Why 30 days and then it's stopping now?" And the Lord showed me very clearly. He said, "In those 30 days I turned the gift on full blast so that you would experience the full potential of this gift. And now I'm going to turn the gift off." Why? Because He wanted to teach me how to stir it up; how to activate it; how to turn it on and turn it off. I learned that this is a gift we are not supposed to have "on" all the time.

Revelation 1:10 says that John was "in the Spirit on the Lord's day." That implies that he wasn't in the Spirit all the time. So there are times when we should move into the Spirit, and there are times when we should relate to one another on a simpler, more natural basis. Other-wise, people may become nervous wondering what we "see" in them or around them or coming out of them.

Human Pin Cushions

One of the common sights Jonathan sees when he looks into the invisible world is people who look like human pin cushions, walking around with objects such as swords, arrows, or spears protruding from their bodies. These objects represent negative or harmful issues or conditions the people are suffering under. Sometimes he sees words written on the objects that identify the specific problem—words such as "depression," "unforgiveness," "bitterness," "resentment," "fear," "rejection," and the like. He remembers one woman in particular who had eight-foot spears piercing her body in the spirit.

> By this time I had seen a lot of things, but the Lord had started to teach me that these objects had to do with physical healings. One of the key verses was Proverbs 12:18.

Proverbs 12:18: "Reckless words pierce like a sword, but the tongue of the wise brings healing" (NIV).

I said, "Lord, give me the tongue of the wise."

One night during one of my meetings a lady came down and sat in a chair near where I was praying for healing. She looked like a pin cushion. She had spears in the spirit that stuck out 8 to 10 feet in every direction. Each spear had a word written on it: "fear," "rejection," "unforgiveness," "bitterness." As I got close to her I asked, as I always do, "May I lay hands on you to pray?" For the first and only time in my experience, she said, "No, please don't." It turned out that simply touching her caused her physical pain. So then I asked, "Well, may I tell you what I'm seeing?" I described the spears I saw piercing her body.

She said, "Well, that makes sense, because I'm on all these medications for fibromyalgia, chronic fatigue, Epstein-Barr virus, and social anxiety disorders as well." The cumulative effect of all these things was such that whenever anyone got within 8 to 10 feet of her, she could feel it in her body.

The best way I can describe it is that I was seeing in the spiritual what was reflected in the physical. I said to her, "Honey, let me pray for you. Let's remove these spears." And so we began to pray through prayers of forgiveness, and releasing those people who had hurt her. We prayed for about an hour and a half, and after we were done she got up and gave me a great big hug. A short time later, doctors confirmed as well that she was completely healed.

I once asked Jonathan why he did all that praying and why he couldn't simply reach over and pull each spear out. His answer revealed not only his confidence in spiritual authority but also his heart of compassion for the welfare of the whole person.

That's a great question, because some people have done that. But the wound is still there. If you pull out the object but don't deal with the wound it caused, the person in the spirit is still bleeding and wounded. You can pull it out with authority, but what is really needed is to deal with the heart issues. That's where true healing takes place.

Baby Time

Not everything that Jonathan sees in the Spirit about people is negative. Sometimes he sees something that indicates a blessing that is soon to come for the person or people involved. He particularly enjoys it when his discernment has to do with children. He explains:

Sometimes when I look at a young couple I will see in the Spirit a little boy or a little girl, perhaps standing next to the woman, or holding her hand. The couple, of course, sees nothing, but I see it in the Spirit. I usually then ask them if they want to have children or are trying to have children. Many times they tell me that they are trying to have a child but cannot. Physically there is some obstacle that is preventing conception. In many cases where I have prayed for these couples, they ended up having a child of the same gender I saw in the Spirit beforehand. The first time this happened, it stretched me quite a bit in the Spirit, but now I find it quite exciting.

A New Mantle

Jonathan's walk in the invisible realm was raised to a new level when he visited Brazil and received prayer from an anointed worship leader.

I was standing near the front row and suddenly saw on the stage two 15-foot angels never seen before.

When the worship leader prayed over me, he prayed a very simple prayer: "Lord, give him what I have that he would see more in the Spirit." That was it. Then he went to start worship. I was standing near the front row and suddenly saw on the stage two 15-foot angels like I'd never seen before. They were surrounded by fire that came out of them about six feet. At that moment I was *not* thinking, "Oh, this is wonderful." I was thinking, "I'm scared out of my mind! I need to get away from this!" But in the very moment I was thinking to run, I saw the angel closest to me start to walk towards me. He put his hand out, touched my chest, and I hit the floor, curled up in a ball. I felt something like fire cover my body. There I was, dressed in nice clothes, lying on a dusty cement floor in Brazil, drenched in a pool of sweat, and covered with fire in the Spirit. From that posture I began to see things in the audience.

I saw smaller angels, the size of a person, with fire coming out of them about a foot. They were joining in with the worship. The crowd of worshipers looked like they were on fire. As I continued to watch, I saw a dark cloud roll in over the meeting. My first thought was, "That must be bad." But then I realized that the presence of the Lord was in the cloud. I said to myself, "I'll have to look that up later," and I did. Throughout Exodus and Deuteronomy God often revealed His presence to His people with a dark cloud. I saw the Father show up in this meeting, and tremendous healings broke out during that day.

While I was lying on the floor observing all of this, I heard in my heart the words, "new mantle." Then I felt water splashed across my chest. It sounded and felt so real in the natural that I started looking at the front row, thinking, "Who's splashing water on me?"

Later I caught up with the worship leader and said, "Okay, I'm going to be a little scientific here; you tell me what you saw tonight." I asked him to share first because I wanted to confirm what I had seen that evening. He proceeded to share with me everything I just described, but he also added that, "the angel, when he touched me, threw a mantle over me. It had fire coming off the top and water dripping off the bottom, which was the water I felt splashing across me."

Healed of Ovarian Cancer

One significant manifestation of the "new mantle" that Jonathan received in Brazil was that he began to witness miraculous healings at a higher level than before. He remembers in particular praying for an elderly woman who was dying of cancer.

Last summer I was in Washington State and got a call about a lady who was 83 years old and dying of stage four ovarian cancer. They asked if I would come and pray, so I drove out to see her. She had just started her second round of chemotherapy. Not long before, she had had her ovary removed, and the surgeons closed her back up and told her, "We got 90 percent of it, but the other 10 percent we can't operate on. You have four months to live. Go home. Do the chemo, but it's not going to help. You're too old."

I talked with her and said:

"You know, the Lord will take you home, but He wants to take you home with dignity. He doesn't want to take you home with cancer. That's not how the Lord works when He takes people home."

So we agreed together in prayer. There were some objects in the Spirit that we prayed through, particularly some forgiveness prayers and some prayers about fear for her grandkids. We prayed those through for about an hour, but didn't see anything tremendous happen at that moment. Two weeks later she called me. She had been to her doctor and he had come in with her chart and said, "I don't quite know how to tell you this, but you're 100 percent cancer free."

You Too Can Learn to Discern

Jonathan Welton wants you to know that even though he walks at a high level of discernment and prophetic insight, this doesn't mean that he is somebody special or some kind of "super Christian." He is an ordinary person who has been touched by an extraordinary God. Just as God has a specific purpose for Jonathan's life, He has a specific purpose for your life, too. And just as Jonathan has learned and grown in the gift of discerning of spirits, you can as well. The gift of discernment is available to every believer. It is part of the "solid food" of spiritual maturity. Hebrews 5:14 says, *"Solid food is for the mature, who by constant use have trained themselves to distinguish (discern) good from evil"* (NIV). Furthermore, John counsels us not to *"believe every spirit, but test the spirits to see whether they are from God"* (1 John 4:1 NIV). Testing the spirits is the definition of discernment, and John's instruction applies to everyone who follows Messiah Yeshua. Every believer is supposed to exercise wise and careful discernment. Just as we have five natural senses—sight, smell, taste, touch, and hearing—we also have five spiritual senses. Sight is one of those five, so we should all be able to discern spirits to one degree or another.

Do you want to increase your qualities of discernment? You can have...

...the gift of discernment because it is part of your heritage as a child of God.

He is your Father, so ask Him. Ask your heavenly Father for greater discernment that you may exercise it for His glory and for the good of others.

Prayer of Impartation

Jonathan's story of being literally set apart from birth is amazing. It really demonstrates the special commission that God has for him. God's plan for each one of us is unique and God longs for all of us to walk in the fullness of our calling. Do you know what your specific purpose in life is?

Jonathan describes receiving an impartation through a prophetic word that helped him solidify his identity and calling.

His life changed when someone saw the diamond in the rough and called his spiritual gifts into reality (see Rom. 4:17).

The Bible encourages us to eagerly seek spiritual gifts and God will show us the most excellent way to follow after Him (see 1 Cor. 12:31). The gift of discernment is part of your heritage as a believer and is the mark of a mature believer (see Heb. 5:14). I'm going to pray that the spiritual gifts in you are called to the surface in your life.

> Father, I speak to those reading this book and call forth their spiritual gifts. I thank You that You've got a specific purpose and plan for their life, and I pray that You would stir their gifts.

> I thank You, Father, that when we ask for a gift from You, You are a good Dad who gives us good gifts (see Luke 11:13). I pray that You would release each reader into a deeper level of understanding how their unique spiritual gifts work.

> Jonathan experienced 30 days of open vision as a seer that acted as a training ground for him. I pray that these readers will embark on their own journey of training. I pray that they will learn how to use their gifts with wisdom and guidance from You. I pray that they would build the Kingdom of God with their gifts and lead others to You through them.

> Friends, I declare to you that your spiritual gifts and calling are not based on your good works, and cannot be taken back (see Rom. 11:29). God has called and equipped you according to His purpose (see Rom. 8:28).

You are called heavenward, to peace, and to holiness (see Phil. 3:14; Col. 3:15; 2 Tim. 1:9). I pray that you would grow in your revelation of who you are and what God has empowered you to do with your life. Amen.

For information about Jonathan's ministry, please visit www.JonWelton.com.

Chapter Eight

A Radical Encounter with Jesus

Todd White knows from firsthand experience the life-transforming power of Messiah Jesus. Raised in a broken home and frequently in trouble, he was a drug addict by the age of 12. One night, during a drug deal gone bad, Todd was shot multiple times at close range, yet every bullet missed. It was almost as though he had an invisible shield protecting him. Perhaps he did, for he then heard a supernatural voice speaking to him. Shortly after this he had a radical encounter with Jesus three days in a row that changed his life forever. Now he walks in supernatural power, even approaching complete strangers on the street and praying for their healing—with amazing results. Like Todd, you too can be changed. Let Todd's story inspire you to allow Jesus to touch your life radically, too.

Life didn't start out very promising for Todd White. His parents divorced when he was very young. His mother worked three jobs to make ends meet. Todd's childhood behavior was so rowdy and uncontrollable that at one point he was sent to a boys' home. At the age of 11½ he started using drugs, and by the time he was 12, he was getting high frequently. His drug use continued to escalate and he became an addict. He was a drug addict for 22 years. Todd even joined the Marine Corps, but ended up going AWOL. As a result, he was dismissed from the service with a bad conduct discharge and even spent some time in prison. One night he met a young woman at a bar. They lived together for nine years and had a daughter. He was a drug-dealing, drug-addicted atheist. Then came the night when everything began to change. It didn't happen overnight, but God got his attention. As Todd remembers:

> I went out looking for drugs one night. The problem was that I didn't have any money. I was actually a Christian at this point, having asked Jesus to come into my heart about five and a half months prior. But I had never gotten into the Word and did not understand how it could transform me in my relationship with Jesus. So that night I was looking for some crack, and I picked up this kid on a back street. Once I had the drugs in my hand, I told him that I was a police officer and started to read him his rights. He freaked out.

> I pulled over and stopped and told him to step out of the car and put his hands on the hood. As soon as he got out of the car, I hit the gas. He unloaded a large pistol at me. I don't know how many bullets he fired but I know it was enough that I shouldn't be here right now. At that moment, I heard a voice…

...I heard an audible voice say to me, "I took those bullets for you. Are you ready to live for Me yet?"

I actually did the drugs I had stolen, but didn't get high that night. It was really weird because they were very real drugs. I had smoked crack and I knew what they were. Since I didn't get high, I went back home. My girlfriend was there, and by this time in our relationship she hated me. She was ready for me to leave. She was an atheist also, as I had been, but since I had become a Christian I had never really represented Jesus to her. I had never tried to tell her that she needed Jesus. She told me that I needed to leave. "You know," I said to her, "I actually do need to leave." That very night, I left the house. Three days later, I entered Teen Challenge in Harrisburg, Pennsylvania, where I stayed for two months. During that time I had a radical encounter with Jesus three nights in a row.

Man on the Street

Before that encounter, however, Todd suffered from nightmares. From the day he entered Teen Challenge he had to deal with bad dreams. He explains:

I had horrible nightmares every night. Every time I went to sleep I was attacked in my dreams. It was the only place where satan had access to my soul—my mind, will and emotions. Because I had these nightmares on a nightly basis, it wasn't long before my roommates became freaked out by me. I would run around the room screaming and yelling, and then hide under the bed. It was horrible.

One day I was sitting across the street from the Teen Challenge induction center in Harrisburg. I had my guitar with me, and even though I didn't know how to play, I just sat there strumming the strings. A homeless man came up pushing a shopping cart. He was wearing army fatigues and sneakers. Oddly enough, he also had swim goggles on his head. He was a real character, the kind of person Jesus said we are supposed to love and not just walk past. So I looked at him and said, "Man, do you know how much Jesus loves you?"

He pulled his shopping cart closer to me and said, "Yes, I do. Do you know how much He loves *you*?" Then he started to talk to me and told me that I had a demon. He didn't know me or where I was from, yet he knew something about me that he could not have known by natural means. There was another member of the Teen Challenge program with me, and the homeless man told him he had a demon too. That made my companion angry, and he walked across the street because he didn't want to hear it. But I didn't get upset. I wanted to hear more. At that time I was still new to the faith and did not understand what words of knowledge were or anything like that. I had no idea. This man started preaching the gospel to me like I had never heard before.

"Man, why are you out here?" I asked him. "Why aren't you preaching somewhere?" He replied, "Twenty years ago, the Lord told me to pick up my cross and follow Him, and I've been pushing this shopping cart across the nation from mission to mission talking to anybody who would listen." His cart was filled with Bibles. Then he said, "We are going to pray, and this thing will not touch you; it will leave you."

He prayed and I didn't feel anything. I went back into the center, where some of the others made fun of me because I was talking to the homeless guy across the street. But when I turned around he wasn't there. I had no idea where he went. All I know is that I went back in there and my life seemed to be the same as before, and I went through the rest of my day. That night I had a dream where I was in a valley with a broad bottom and steep sides. Suddenly, everything started shaking, and I thought the demons were coming to chase me again. Instead, I heard a voice say, "Do not fear, I will never leave you nor forsake you. I will always be with you."

Immediately I woke up. I got up and went into the prayer room where I went every day. When I entered Teen Challenge I made a commitment to pray in the prayer room every day. If there really was a God, I was going to find Him. At that time the Bible was still largely hidden to me. I didn't understand it. I had suffered with ADHD my whole life, and had never read a book before. About six weeks into the program, the Bible became the first book that I could understand. It also happened to be the most important book for me to understand. I opened the Bible to Psalm 23 and read the words, *"Even though I walk through the valley of the shadow of death, I will fear no evil, for you are with me; your rod and your staff, they comfort me"* (Ps. 23:4 NIV).

It suddenly dawned on me, "That's God! This was God talking to me!"

I went through the next day without saying anything to anybody about my dream. That night I had the same dream again. And again, on the third night, but this time it was different.

The third night was really amazing because this time a light followed behind me the whole way down this valley. A voice spoke to me from within the light and I felt something like a hand on my shoulder. The voice said,

"Do not fear. I will never leave you nor forsake you. I'm always with you. This addiction will never touch you again. Go home and restore your relationships with friends and family." I woke up, and it was true. I was free of my addiction. I knew it was time to go home, even though I had only been there a couple of months and had not finished the Teen Challenge program. The thing about Teen Challenge is that you have access to leave. It's an open door. They also understand that it is not the program that changes you, but Jesus through the program who changes you.

A Transformed Family

When Todd left Teen Challenge, he returned home to his girlfriend and their daughter, where he discovered that things were already starting to change for the better. As Todd recalls:

My girlfriend had started on the road to Jesus even before I entered Teen Challenge. While I was there she gave herself fully to the belief that God could transform me. So she came to Jesus, I came home, and we got married four days later in the middle of a church service.

God is so amazing! Today I have the most incredible wife and we have the most incredible marriage. We have never been closer. My wife is absolutely amazing and I love her with all my heart. The Bible says that a husband is to love his wife like Jesus loved the church, and that is an unconditional love.

As for my daughter, who never knew her father except as a drug addict, God has by His amazing grace and mercy enabled her to never look back, but only forward. Anytime we do look back it is only under the covering of the blood of Jesus as a testimony of what He has done for us. Destiny now knows that her dad always keeps his word, never lies, and always follows through with everything (at least I try to). She understands that God has completely transformed not just her daddy, but her life, and her mommy's life. Since that time Zoey, our youngest, has joined the family. Both girls accompany me frequently when I pray for people in stores and other public places. In fact, we pray for them together.

Spirit-Filled "Chutzpah"

Todd's encounter with the strange homeless man on the street that day bears many earmarks of an angelic visitation. The apparent randomness of the encounter, the word of knowledge that was given, the sudden disappearance of the man afterward; all these suggest that the fatigues-clad, goggle-wearing man pushing the shopping cart may have been a heavenly messenger. Whether or not this is so, one thing seems certain: Todd received an impartation of love that day that has since manifested in amazing instances of miracles, words of knowledge, and healing. After living for the devil for so many years as a drug addict, he lives exclusively for God now. He goes out on the streets to minister to people because he loves people. He will even walk up to complete strangers to lay hands on them and pray. He has a Spirit-driven holy boldness; a Spirit-filled "chutzpah," if you will. *Chutzpah* is a Hebrew word that means "nerve." Todd once had nerve for the devil; now he has nerve for God. And many people, often perfect strangers, are blessed as a result. Here is one example, in Todd's own words.

I was getting ready to speak at a church in Richmond, Virginia. It was my first day there. I already had my lapel mic on, ready to preach and share whatever God had put in my heart. The pastor was introducing me and was almost ready to turn the service over to me when I heard a voice in my heart say, not audibly, but as a thought in my mind, "Run out of the church now."

So I ran out. The people were looking around, puzzled, like they were thinking, "Okay, where is he going? What's going on?" I went down to the corner and saw a man coming across the street in a wheelchair. After he got across I said to him, "Hey buddy, how are you?"

"I'm okay," he said. "What do you want?"

I said, "I don't want anything. I just see that you're in a wheelchair. Why are you in it?"

He replied, "Back in 1976 I fell off a bridge and shattered my leg." As a result, he had two steel rods extending from his thigh to his shin bone, one on each side of his knee, to hold his leg together. Over the years his knee had grown solid with calcium the whole way through because he couldn't bend his leg.

"God can heal your knee," I told him.

"Well, I don't believe that," he replied.

I said, "I'm not interested in whether you believe it or not. I'm not trying to tell you that you have to believe what I'm saying to you. Let me *show* you. Let me pray for your knee."

Then he said, "I fell and broke my ribs a couple days ago, and I'm in severe pain."

"Then let me pray for your ribs, okay?"

"Don't touch my ribs," he pleaded.

I reached in, placed my hand gently on his ribs, and said, "In Jesus' name, ribs, I command you be healed right now." All of a sudden he just looked at me and his eyes got really big. I said, "Move your ribs around…"

…He looked at me in shock. "All the pain is gone!" His ribs came together right then and there.

Now the man was a little less combative. I said to him, "Come on, man, you've got to let me pray for your knee."

"It won't change anything," he insisted, but not so much in a fighting tone but almost like a question.

So I prayed for his knee. All this time my lapel mic had been live, and the people in the church, having heard all of this conversation, started coming outside. I finished praying...and nothing happened. The man just looked at me and said, "I told you so."

I prayed again, and he bent his leg a tiny bit. And then the third and the fourth time I just kept hitting it and hitting it and hitting it with prayer. The Word of God is like a hammer. You pound on that thing and keep on pounding. Suddenly, his knee bent all the way and he freaked out.

"I've never seen it do that before!" he said in astonishment. "It can't bend! There's metal in there!" He stood up and got out of the wheelchair, but his back was bent over.

"What's wrong with your back?" I asked.

He replied, "I broke my back when I fell."

His knee was now working, so I prayed for his back. And he stood straight up right there on the street corner. He bent over and touched the ground with his hands. Then he walked...for the first time in over 30 years.

But what about those metal rods? I asked Todd how the man could bend his knee with those metal rods in place.

We have prayed for people who have gone back to the doctor and discovered that the metal is gone; it simply is not there anymore. That's a real good way to get to a doctor's heart, especially if he or she is the one who inserted the metal in the first place.

Signs Follow Those Who *Believe*

Many Christians fail to pray with confidence for the sick because they are afraid of what might happen if it doesn't work. Will the faith of the person being prayed for be damaged or even destroyed by their failure to be healed? Will the person praying for healing be rejected or ridiculed for the same failure? If you are praying for someone on *God's* behalf, it is impossible for them to reject *you*. His love never fails. Besides, what happens if they *do* get healed? Some Christians pray for the sick but "hedge their bets," so to speak, by keeping a "cop out" ready at hand. If no healing occurs, they simply say that the person being prayed for did not have enough faith. But how much is "enough"? Jesus said that faith the size of a mustard seed can move a mountain (see Matt. 17:20). So how much faith is necessary for healing?

Todd sees things differently. In fact, he believes that dwelling on the faith of the person being prayed for is the wrong focus. More important, he says, is the faith of the person praying.

Mark 16:17-18 says:

And these signs will accompany those who believe: In my name they will drive out demons; they will speak in new tongues...they will place their hands on sick people, and they will get well (NIV).

Notice that it says, "These signs will accompany those who *believe*." It doesn't say, "These signs will accompany those being prayed for." It is the believing believer—the one who is praying—who is responsible fully and completely for a person being healed. I can't afford to depend on *their* faith. How are we going to touch witches? How are we going to touch Muslims? How are we going to touch Hindus? I don't want to run from these people. I love them. I want to hug them because I know that God will touch them."

Todd sums up this perspective with a simple statement:

"My faith trumps their unbelief."

Todd's faith is outrageous. In fact, his faith is outrageously *normal*. Every believer should walk in this kind of faith. Faith to move mountains (and to heal the sick) should be normal for us. It should be normal for you. And it can be normal for you. If you are afraid that you don't have that kind of faith, ask the Lord to increase your faith. Like the desperate father who sought Jesus' healing for his demon-possessed son, cry out to God, *"Lord, I believe; help my unbelief!"* (Mark 9:24 NKJV). He will.

Remember—Jesus didn't just pay a price to get you into heaven. He paid a price to get heaven into you. Through the Holy Spirit, heaven should flow through you daily to destroy hell and set the captives free. Don't just go *to* the church. *Be* the church!

Prayer of Impartation

Todd has an incredible testimony of salvation and deliverance. He received an impartation of love from a homeless man, and God granted him faith for miracles and the gift of words of knowledge. Even Todd's children were protected from Todd's actions.

The miraculous life is also part of our heritage as believers. Healing is easy, and it is not dependent on the person prayed for, but rather, on the person praying. Todd encourages us to exercise great faith while praying and to remember that our faith for miracles and healings trumps the unbelief of those we pray for.

The same anointing that is on Todd's life is available to you. Turn your heart toward God and pray with me.

Father, I ask you for a greater boldness and courage to pray for those around me who need healing and miracles. I offer my hands to you. Use me God. Use me to heal the sick, to raise the dead, to demonstrate your goodness through miracles, signs, and wonders. Teach me your ways, God. Show me how to walk in the supernatural. Give me revelation about how to pray for the sick. Lord, I'm willing; teach me. Amen.

Todd shared that praying for people is like using a hammer—pray the word of God, and hammer it into a situation. Do you need courage to step out and talk to people you don't know? Know that if God's presence is leading you to pray for someone, He has already prepared a miracle for them. When you begin to focus your heart on God in public places, you shift the atmosphere and agree with Heaven's heart for that place. You literally bring Heaven to Earth (see Matt. 6:10). Allow the Holy Spirit to coach you in discerning where He's moving and who He wants to touch.

In Heaven, miracles are reality. You are bringing that superior reality to earth. It's a miracle. It's normal.

Father, thank you for your sons and daughters. Jesus come into their life right now.

I release a breakthrough anointing over your life to pray for the sick. You will have authority over cancer, mental illness, digestive disorders, and all diseases that affect muscles, bones, organs, and the blood. Your words will shift the spiritual atmosphere and bring heavenly realities to earth. You will access the spare parts room and see kneecaps grow back and other body parts "replaced" by God Himself. You will impart divine healing to people. When you lay hands on people in prayer, the fire of God will fall on people and cause them to know and understand the awe-inspiring reverence of God. People will encounter the living God through your ministry. Signs and wonders will follow you because you believe.

For information about Todd's ministry, please visit www.neckministries.com.

Chapter Nine

ANGELS IN THE NIGHT

Over 15 years ago, Steven Brooks had a heavenly encounter with an angel, and he's been communicating with angels ever since. Have you ever wondered why angels appear to some people but not to others? Do you need victory in your life? Are you wondering what lies ahead for our country? Read Steven's story and you will find answers to all these questions. You will discover an ancient form of victory that few people really understand and grasp. You will learn about the new miracles that are coming to America. Be inspired and watch your faith grow as Steven shares the insights and revelations he has received from his supernatural encounters with angels.

Few people are ever blessed in life to hear the audible voice of God. Steven Brooks is one of those few. It happened 18 years ago, the first of numerous notable encounters he has had with the supernatural in the years following. This first experience set his life in a new direction and set the stage for deeper experiences to come. Steven explains:

I was down in Mississippi at my grandmother's house. She was a very godly woman. At the time of my encounter nobody else was home. My family, my brothers, and my grandmother had all gone up the hill to do something. I spent my time in one of the rooms of the house, alone, just reading my Bible. After a while, I lay down on the floor and started praying. Before long I heard an audible male voice that said, *"Draw near to God, and He will draw near to you"* (James 4:8).

At that time I did not know that the words the voice spoke were from the Bible. About two weeks later I was reading the Book of James and came across James 4:8, which says, *"Draw near to God and He will draw near to you."* That was the first of many similar types of experiences that began to propel and push me to the desire to have a deeper walk with God.

I started running with this information, even though I didn't understand really how to draw near to God. But I began to take small steps; the basics. I began to study the Bible more, read the Bible more, and pray more. I began to wait on the Lord, and over time, by His grace, I began to make some spiritual progress.

Steven continued to grow in his faith, in his prayer life, and in his understanding of Scripture until, some years later, while on an extended fast, he had an even more powerful and memorable supernatural visitation. As he recalls:

In the year of 2000 I was doing a 40-day fast with just water and occasionally some thin apple juice just to give me some energy. On the tenth day of the fast, when I was in my office alone, the Lord came into the office. He didn't come in the form of a person, but as a ball of light that came out from the ceiling and hovered in the corner of the room. Out of that light, out of that ball of glory, the Lord spoke to me. He said, "Take a pen and a notepad, and write one through seven." I grabbed a pen and notepad as fast as I could and wrote down the numbers one through seven. Then He said, "Write these down; these seven waves of blessing will come upon your life." After I had written them all down, I looked at them and realized they provided a blueprint for the plan that God had for me, for my personal life as well as for my ministry.

People have asked me why God would show me these things this way. After all, an encounter like mine is pretty rare. The only thing I can say is that He did it to help me because I really wanted to know His will and plan for my life. I didn't want just to try plan A or plan B; I wanted to go for the gold standard. I was asking, "Lord what is it you want me to accomplish in my life?" That's what I wanted to focus on, so when He gave me that blueprint, I had things I could look at to help me know the direction to go. It was a faith project, and I could see that the Lord wanted to fulfill these things. In the years since, I have seen them starting to come to pass.

A Semi-Circle of Angels

Not only has Steven Brooks received angelic visitations; on one occasion he was visited by *five* angels at once! Their message to him had to do with revival. Steven recalls the encounter:

> I woke up at 3:00 one morning with a sense that something was about to happen. Like David in the Old Testament hearing the rustling in the mulberry trees, I knew something was about to happen in the realm of the spirit, some type of visitation (see 2 Sam. 5:23-24). But at the same time, honestly, I was tired. After all, it was 3:00 in the morning. So after getting up and praying for about 15 minutes, I decided to lie down again for a little bit, and leaned back on the bed. At 3:30 I suddenly sat straight up, totally awake. I know what time it was because I glanced at the clock. Straight in front of me, at the foot of the bed, five angels were standing in a semi-circle. All of them were looking at me and smiling.

> In appearance they looked absolutely glorious; beautiful creatures with no imperfections at all. They said to me, "We are the five angels of revival." When they said that, I understood that they were not the *only* angels of revival. These five particular angels had stood with five particular men during previous revivals in church history. One of them, in fact, was associated with a revival that was taking place in the church at the time of this visitation.

People ask, "Why five angels?" I don't really know for sure. But the number five represents grace, so perhaps there was that element of grace there, not that I deserve it. And each one represented a great revival of the past or present, and had ministered to men who were the principal figures or leaders in those revivals.

The Spirit of Holiness

The five angels that visited Steven Brooks at 3:30 in the morning came to talk to him about revival. More specifically, they came to talk to him about the greatest key to revival for a church or an individual: the importance of holy living. Steven explains:

> They said to me, "We want to talk with you about the spirit of holiness." For the next 30 minutes they did most of the talking. I was allowed to ask a few questions, but for half an hour they told me how important it is to live a life that is pleasing to the Lord with holiness. They stressed that each individual believer has a responsibility to do his or her part. Some people define holiness as an external thing that has to do with the way you dress, or the particular things you do or don't do. That may be part of it, but holiness is first internal, a condition of the heart. There was no trace of what we would call legalism in what the angels told me, or phrases like, "You can't do this," or "You can't do that." In our heart we know the Holy Spirit will lead us to do things that are pleasing to the Lord. At the same time,

our external behavior is important because there are certain things that we don't want to put into our ears. There are certain things that we don't want our eyes to see. We want to maintain purity as much as possible, because that also will attract the angels.

In the spirit realm, angels pick up on an impure thought life.

They are able to see what we are emanating; what is radiating out of us.

I asked Steven if he was talking about things like watching violent or suggestive television and other things of that sort, or whether he was referring to something much deeper.

Those types of things bring a kind of spiritual defilement. We may think, "This doesn't affect me," but in the spirit realm, these things are very easily distinguished. Angels can tell what a person is emanating. If you are emanating the love of God and a life of purity, they want to be around you. Such things attract them…

...Evil spirits are attracted to impurity.

They, too, can tell what a person is emanating. If you fill your mind with all sorts of garbage and filth, they will gather around that. Thoughts of self-centeredness, depression, impurity, immorality, and the like draw them. So there is a way that we need to live that is holy and pleasing to the Lord, to create an atmosphere that is conducive to the Holy Spirit.

One of the keys to holy living is a spirit of humility. This, too, is something Steven learned during his visitation by the five angels of revival.

One of the angels appeared to me to be one of the most humble beings I have ever seen in my life, so I surmised that the man he stood with during revival must have been extremely humble. So I asked the angel, "What was it like to be in a full-blown move of God's Spirit during the revival that you ministered in?" He replied, "Really, we didn't have much to do with it; we gave all the glory to God; He carried the whole thing." That angel just deflected everything right back on the Lord. I knew then that the man whom he helped stand with in ministry must have been an extremely humble man. It reminded me of what the Book of Numbers says about Moses, that he was the most humble man on the face of the earth (see Num. 12:3). So there's somebody today that actually is the most humble person on the face of the earth.

God measures success completely differently from the way man does. We look at numbers, power, money, and influence. God looks at obedience and humility. Success in God's eyes is to humble ourselves before him and to be obedient to Him, doing whatever He has told us to do, whatever it might be. That is where the spiritual anointing comes from, and where the reward lies.

Holy Ghost Revival

During that same angelic visitation, Steven received a taste of what genuine revival is like.

Right at the end, just before they left, the angels asked me a question: "Would you like to experience what it is like to be under that power of the Holy Spirit in a full-blown move of God's Spirit, a Holy Ghost revival?" They actually used that old-fashioned term. Without hesitation I said, "Yes! Absolutely!" This was no time to go back to bed! When I said that, each one of those angels reached out with his right hand and touched me very gently with the tip of his index finger.

I fell out for two hours. It was like being hooked up to some kind of electrical current that shot all through my body. I suddenly lost all strength and fell off the bed.

The fall didn't hurt; I wasn't bruised or anything, but for the next two hours I was shaking all over. My mind was still working the whole time this was going on, and I thought for sure I would wake up my wife and daughter, who were sleeping in the next room. (I had left the room to go into a separate room to pray.)

It was one of those things you just yield to; it was the Lord doing a work.

He was doing a deeper work in me. He was shaking more of Steven Brooks out, so there could be more of God to fill me up. It was a deeper surrender to the Lord, a deeper letting go, a deeper level of my saying to Him, "I'll do anything, and I really mean it, as much as I can possibly and sincerely express that." It was laying aside more of myself to make more room for him.

The Coming Healing Revival

We've already seen how the Lord visited Steven on the tenth day of a 40-day fast and gave him a seven-point "blueprint" for his life and ministry. There was more to that supernatural encounter, however. The Lord went on to reveal to Steven details concerning a great healing revival that is coming soon to America. Steven explains:

> During my fast, on that tenth day, the Lord spoke to me about a coming healing revival that will be the greatest movement in history of God's Spirit bringing healing and miracles. In fact, in some ways it is already beginning to break upon the church. One of the things the Lord told me about this revival is that it is America's turn. There are some great things coming. The Lord has provoked the American church to jealousy. We've heard about the great miracles, even the creative miracles, in South America, in Africa, and in different parts of the world, but we've only seen little tidbits of that here in America. But that is coming to our shores. These great creative miracles are coming to America, and a healing revival is going to hit a level that will surpass anything that's ever happened in church history. It's going to be very powerful.
>
> For example, the Lord said that when this revival comes, meetings will run around the clock: 24 hours a day, 7 days a week. There will be a total outpouring of His Spirit. He even spoke to me of specific kinds of

miracles. People who have suffered severe burns, even third-degree burns, which can even be fatal, will be brought into the meetings, where they will be completely healed and receive brand new skin. The same thing happened to Naaman, the Syrian army general in the Old Testament. He was a leper but he received brand new skin and was made completely whole when he washed seven times in the Jordan River (see 2 Kings 5:1-14). The Bible says his skin became like that of a young child. In this revival we're going to see these types of creative miracles that won't boggle our faith, but will boggle the imagination of many people.

In another example, the Lord told me that children with Down syndrome and people who have suffered mental retardation will come to the meetings and sit under the glory of the Lord. In two weeks they will be completely healed; their minds will be completely restored to them.

I have even had a foretaste of this myself. I have prayed for several people that the Lord has touched—children with Down syndrome. The Lord made their minds whole, and it affected their physical bodies. Their mothers have told me that a miracle has taken place and their children have been healed. So we're already touching on this, pushing into these new realms of healing and creative miracles that the Lord wants to *explode* upon the American church.

Praise: The Lost Key to Victory

At the beginning of this chapter I asked you if you need victory in your life. I know I do. We all do. Victory in daily life is available for every believer and follower of Yeshua, the Messiah, but very few experience it. Why? Steven learned a critical key to victory that most believers either do not know or have forgotten. The Lord revealed this key to him using two instances of lost keys. Steven explains:

> I had two similar experiences occur in my life that for a couple of years were very perplexing to me. On two separate occasions I lost my keys. I *never* lose keys, but on these two occasions I did. The first was years ago, before the Lord put me in full-time ministry, when I was working in the plumbing field. I lost my keys and later found them in a most unusual way. Several years went by, and then one day when I was in Moravian Falls, North Carolina helping a friend with a project, I lost my keys again. And once again I found them in a most unusual way. Sometime later I went to northern Virginia to do a revival meeting. I was there for five days. On the last day of that meeting, I was in my hotel room alone. I had one more meeting to do that night. That afternoon I was praying, getting ready for the evening service. My wife and daughter had gone into town to do a few things, so I had the hotel room all to myself. As I sat praying and waiting on the Lord, I was suddenly aware that somebody had come into the room. The whole atmosphere of the room changed. A

male voice spoke to me and said, "This is why you were allowed to find lost keys."

"Praise is the lost key to victory."

Many Christians do not experience a greater degree of victory in their lives because they do not make praise a regular part of their spiritual walk. Praise should be as natural to us as breathing—and just as continual. In fact, for a Christian, praise should be a *lifestyle*. Praise opens access to the blessings of Heaven. As an example, Steven shares the story of a woman with a broken foot who praised her way to victory and healing.

This was a great miracle that happened in one of our conferences we hosted recently. A lady flew all the way out from California, believing that if she got to the meeting, God would do a miracle in her foot. She had five broken bones in her foot, and an X-ray to prove it. But she also had faith for healing. She came into the meeting on crutches, but also brought a pair of tennis shoes to wear afterwards. That's how strong her faith was. She knew God was going to heal her.

I prayed for her that afternoon, the last day of the meeting. It was late in the afternoon, and we had one more session that evening. During the last praise and worship song of that meeting, guess who came dancing down the aisle in front of hundreds of people, with a brand new, healed foot? This lady returned to her doctor in California, who reexamined her foot. He then informed her that instead of five bones, she had broken seven. Then he held up the latest X-ray and said, "I've never seen such phenomenal new bone growth development." The X-ray shows white streaks that shot out from the broken bones, showing where the new bones instantly grew back out. She was completely healed. And all because she believed the Lord for her healing and *praised* Him for it even before it happened.

What About You?

Has Steven's story stirred a desire in you for supernatural encounters of your own? Do you long for angels to visit you as they do him? There is nothing wrong with such desires, Steven says, but he offers a word of caution. Do not seek supernatural encounters or angelic visitations for their own sake. That's the wrong focus. Instead, seek the Lord Himself, who is the initiator of such encounters. Do you remember when Steven heard an audible voice saying, "Draw near to God and He will draw near to you"? The Lord offers the same counsel to you. If you want the Lord to be close to you, draw close to Him. But you must approach Him in humility, with a submissive spirit that is ready to hear, learn, and obey. This is the key not only to intimacy with God, but also to spiritual victory.

If you want to be closer to God, spend more time with Him. Read, meditate on, and study His Word. Open up your heart to Him in prayer...

...wait on Him expectantly, with your heart and mind tuned to hear His voice.

The Lord honors and rewards those who wait humbly and expectantly on Him. Hebrews 11:6 says, *"And without faith it is impossible to please Him, for he who comes to God must believe that He is and that **He is a rewarder of those who seek Him"*** (NASB, emphasis added). The prophet Jeremiah announces this promise from the Lord:

> *"For I know the plans that I have for you," declares the Lord, "plans for welfare and not for calamity to give you a future and a hope. Then you will call upon Me and come and pray to Me, and I will listen to you. You will seek Me and find Me when you search for Me with all your heart"* (Jeremiah 29:11-13 NASB).

If you want to know God's heart, love Him with all your heart. Spend time in His presence. Psalm 25:14 says, *"The secret of the Lord is for those who fear Him, And He will make them know His covenant"* (NASB).

The Lord has promised to draw near to you if you draw near to Him. Don't delay; do it today. Start right now. Take that first step toward a deeper relationship with God. You'll find Him right there waiting for you.

Prayer of Impartation

Steven's testimony of angelic visitations and encounters with God should provoke us all to jealousy. They started when he set himself aside to seek God for divine direction. Steven's holy lifestyle attracted heavenly encounters to him.

I pray that a spirit of holiness would fall on those reading this book. I pray, God, that You would prompt them to yield to You on deeper levels and that holiness would be a lifestyle. I pray for great humility to sustain the move of God that is coming. Lord, I pray that this holiness would attract the angelic activity of Heaven to these believers.

In the name of Jesus, I release an impartation of miracles over you. I release this anointing that Steven has talked about: a powerful move that surpasses what's occurred in church history in the past and that carries an anointing for creative miracles.

I release an anointing over you to pray for fatal third-degree burns to be healed. We agree for total healing, so that those healed will have brand new skin. We thank you for complete restoration for people with Down syndrome—complete healing in Jesus' name.

Thank you, God, for the testimonies of healings we've heard. We want to see a greater move of God in our nation. Lord, come move in our land. We pray that the Kingdoms of our God would become the kingdoms of this world (see Rev. 11:15). Amen.

Steven cautioned us to not get distracted from intimacy with God by seeking the supernatural and miracles for their own sake.

Lord, we thank You that part of our inheritance as believers is the realm of the supernatural and miraculous. But, we don't want to get distracted from our relationship with You. Lord, help us keep things in perspective. Help us build intimacy with you. Thank You that You've given us praise as a key to victory.

Lord, we choose to praise You with all of our hearts, to tell of Your wonders, to lift Your name above all names (see Ps. 9:1). We will sing Your praises, God, and declare to everyone we meet what You have done for us (see Ps. 9:11).

No miracle is greater than You, Jesus. We love and adore You, and You are always the object of our affection. You are our portion forever! (see Ps. 142:5). Lord, as we witness miracles and healings, let them be signs that point to You. Let these signs make us wonder about Your greatness. Thank You for who You are. Amen.

For further information about Steven's ministry, please visit www.stevenbrooks.org.

Chapter Ten

A NEW REFORMATION IS COMING

We first met Jason Westerfield in Chapter 2 when he was featured on Darren Wilson's film about miracles, *The Finger of God.* You will recall Darren's account of how Jason prayed for him to be able to see into the supernatural realm, as well as his testimony of the healing of a homeless man they met on the street. Such encounters are commonplace for Jason, who walks regularly in a high plane of the supernatural. Praying for the healing of perfect strangers is only part of what Jason does. The Lord has given him insight and visions about a coming revolution in energy that will boost national economies, and a new spiritual reformation that will change lives on a global scale. During days filled with much social and spiritual uncertainty, Jason's message should encourage us all in the hope that the future is bright indeed for those who know the Lord. Let Jason's story fill you with confidence for the days that lie ahead.

Among his supernatural experiences, Jason Westerfield has been translated in the Spirit both to the Pentagon and the White House, where he "saw" high-level meetings take place.

He even "saw" President George W. Bush offer Alan Greenspan a second term as chairman of the Federal Reserve—weeks before it was announced in the media. One of the most amazing revelations he has received from the Lord was regarding a comet that was approaching our solar system and would be visible from earth. God revealed this to Jason before NASA was aware of its existence or that it would be visible from earth. As Jason explains:

> The Lord took me in a new experience and showed me a vision of a comet in the heavens. At the time, this particular comet was unknown to NASA or astronomers. Comets are usually cyclic, so astronomers can predict their appearance, but in this experience the Lord showed me a comet going through outer space and said that it was a sign in the heavens of what He was doing in our generation here on earth. He said that in one generation the whole face and expression of Christianity, as well as the world as a whole, was going to change. We are living in a season of reformation. Just as Martin Luther ignited the Protestant Reformation in the early 1500s with the rediscovery that salvation is by the grace of God through faith in Jesus, our generation is going to have a greater understanding of the Kingdom of God. People will walk in greater intimacy with the Lord than ever before and will begin to walk in the greater works of Messiah Jesus.
>
> The sign and wonder of the prophetic word was confirmed a couple of months later and written about in

newspapers. NASA and other astronomers were caught by surprise not expecting to see this comet. The last time this comet was seen in the sky was at the tail end of the Reformation in the early 1600s.

Exciting times lie ahead!

Considering Jason's background growing up, he seems an unlikely candidate to receive such supernatural insights.

But that's the kind of people God likes to use. As a young boy Jason was basically unchurched; his family was not religious. Nevertheless, he had his first supernatural encounter with God while still a young child. In fact, even his experience of coming to know Jesus was out of the ordinary.

I was praying in my room one day, not knowing exactly what prayer was, and I just said, "God, if You are real, would you please come into my room right now?" At the time, my room was completely dark. Suddenly, a bright light shined in my room for about 45 seconds, so bright that it took awhile for my eyes to adjust. Once they did, I saw a man sitting on the floor in a position of prayer. He turned and looked at me with the biggest smile I had ever seen. His eyes were of the brightest intensity and he was surrounded by a living cloud, almost like electricity, that came off of Him and rested on me. My whole body was filled with love. It was like an electrical current, a warm energy that flowed through my whole being. I had never felt so loved in all my life.

Jason never forgot this experience, but as he grew older he set his sights on a show business career in southern California. He soon discovered that the things he thought would bring him success only left him feeling empty. This set him up for a radical encounter with Jesus.

I began to notice that many of the people around me who seemed to be succeeding had lives that were empty. They might have had fame, money, and a lot of good things going for them, but inside was a void.

It was the same with me. I realized that what I thought was success really wasn't, and it was a sad reality for me. Seeking an answer, I began to meditate and pray, knowing there was a God but not knowing exactly what His name was. I began to try to see God the only way I knew how. I then had an encounter once again with the same Person who had entered my room when I was a young boy. Right there in my living room the Lord Jesus appeared to me, and I was radically saved. He told me how much He loved me...

...for the next three and a half weeks, I had supernatural encounters almost daily.

This was before I had even been to church for the first time.

All I had was a Bible, and in it I encountered normal people like me. Many of them, in fact, had worse "résumés" than I did—adulterers, murderers, deceivers—yet God spoke to them. Most of them worked normal jobs and then God worked through them in supernatural feats. When I read about all of this I thought that lifestyle was normal for every believer. Since I had never been to church, I didn't know any better. I saw what God had done in their lives and, realizing that mankind hadn't really changed, and that God was the same, I asked God if these things could take place in my life. He said yes. I started asking Him to show me things that would take place, things related to the weather and to other conditions in the earth. During this time the Lord also began to show me things that were taking place in the business world with mergers and acquisitions. So from the very beginning I didn't have the grid for religion, or the idea that Christianity was something that only took place in a building.

When I finally started going to church I expected to find my experience with God to be typical, but what I saw in the first church I attended really shocked me. A lot of the people seemed depressed, as if weighted down with a heavy burden. I soon discovered that even the ones who seemed happy had not had an encounter anything like mine. I still remember the time when I started sharing out of my friendship with God the things that He was sharing with me and about the great hours that I had with Him, when someone in the church first informed me that "God doesn't speak today." My first thought was, "What planet are you from?" I *know* God speaks today because He spoke to me every day. How can you have a friendship or a relationship with someone that is personal unless you communicate with that person? Try it with your spouse and see!

Spiritual Winds

Jason's insight into the spiritual realm has shown him that activity in the supernatural often manifests as blowing winds in the natural. He explains:

God is the Lord of all creation. He is the Lord of Heaven, and that has to do with atmospheres and environments, as well as the weather. All of these things are under His control. The Bible also says that God turns His angels into winds. Sometimes when the realm of the Kingdom starts coming in, and there is a lot of angelic activity, and the supernatural realm of the Spirit starts unfolding in the natural realm, what we see initially on earth is that winds begin to blow.

I was in Santa Nella, California a few years back and the Lord told me there would be record high winds that day because of angelic activity, as well as numerous miracles. Without my touching anybody, but just welcoming God's Holy Spirit into the room, miracles began taking place. People who were blind received their sight. Tumors were dissolved. Such a powerful range of authority opened up that people over at the local hospital began to get healed as well. Some of them, who already had loved ones there, even came to the meeting. All the while we could hear winds blowing outside, tossing about trash cans and other loose items. Going back to my room later, I had to fight to avoid getting blown over by the wind. The newspaper the next day reported record high winds for Santa Nella.

On another occasion, Jason took the unusual step of bringing the entire congregation outside, where gusting winds accompanied spiritual activity.

There were about 115 of us inside and I sensed the Lord telling me to take everyone outside. I said, "Lord, I don't think they have done that here before." He replied, "Well, that is what I am doing. Do what I am doing." So I said to everyone, "Let's all go outside."

We went out into the parking lot. I didn't touch any-one. Suddenly a circular wind, a whirlwind, started to blow around all the people in the natural. God took off the spiritual blinders and 91 people out of those 115 saw open-eyed visions. These were accountants and house-wives; normal people, not super spiritual people...

...they saw into the heavens right in front of them.

Some saw chariots and others saw angels.

The Coming Economic Revolution

Among the spiritual insights Jason receives regularly are many that have to do with business and economic issues. In fact, one day he received a 40-minute "download" of what God is going to do in the global economy. Here is what he learned:

I was having breakfast with my wife. I wasn't feeling especially spiritual, just enjoying time with my wife, when a vision opened up to my left for about 40 to 45 minutes, in which the Lord began to show me the coming energy revolution. Just as we had an Industrial Age, this generation will be known as the Energy Age. There will be a revolution in energy. We are going to move to a hydrogen-based world economy, and when that begins to come about, geo-political changes will take place, leading to a massive human rights movement on a global scale. In my vision I saw some converters which every nation will be able to utilize and become self-sufficient in their energy. Because of this new development the world will no longer be dependent on oil and we will see literally a global shift in power begin to take place.

I asked Jason what this vision had to say about the United States, with our continuing economic problems.

Well, I know that God isn't mad at America. He loves America. He is the Father not just of America, but of all the nations. If we see the Lord as a Father looking at other nations as His kids, we can understand that He will disciple any nation that comes into alignment with Him and begins to walk in His will and His thoughts and His ways. There are nations right now that are beginning to emerge and finally beginning to succeed and do better than they have before, and because of that they are taking some of the "pie," so to speak, away from America. So it is not that God is mad at America, but that other nations are beginning to succeed. We need to recognize that as Christians we are Kingdom citizens and global citizens. We can invest in these emerging markets, such as New

Zealand, Australia, Brazil, Ukraine, China and India. Why Ukraine? Ukraine is the breadbasket. Ukraine is going to continue to produce a lot of food. With the food it supplies, Ukraine alone could feed most of the world.

Even though the Bible talks about the price of grain being very high in the last days, Jason says that food and commodities are things that God wants believers to invest in.

Over the last two years the Lord has shown me that there is going to be a massive shift of economic power and center. The value of the American dollar will continue to decline because the currencies of other countries are increasing in value. More important than buying the right stock is putting our money in the right place, and if we begin to invest in some of these other currencies, our wealth can multiply and increase.

The commodities market is another important area of investment. Along with the massive economic shift will come a sense of insecurity for many people. People who are afraid don't invest as much, or they shift their investments to "safer" areas. In addition to gold, oil, and precious metals, which continue to be good investments, we need to look also at the commodities, because there will be new highs in a majority of these. In fact, we are starting to see that right now.

It's not that the United States is doing badly as much as it is that third-world countries are starting to do so well. God loves not just America but every nation. He loves the whole world. He is a good Father who wants to see His children succeed, so we are starting to see a great global shift of power and resources. A lot of it is going to go to China and India, which together total about 2.4 billion people: 1.3 billion in China and 1.1 billion in India. That's more than one-third of the world's population. Their production and exports continue to grow and amazing things are going to continue to happen over there.

But is God really interested in these kinds of things? When I asked Jason why God gave him this vision, this was his reply:

Why did He show it? I believe that…

…God is an awesome investor who wants a multiplication of His talents.

The Jewish people as a whole have a natural understanding of finances; that is part of their blessing. If we are going to multiply and increase everything God gives us—not just our gifts and our talents but also our money—we must understand that it is not enough simply to have our money sitting in a bank where it is gradually losing its purchasing power. If that's all we're doing, then we are not multiplying our finances. In the days ahead we are going to have to be discipling nations. God talks about running economies and understanding markets. The Great Commission isn't just about planting churches; it is about discipling nations. So we have to gain understanding of where to position ourselves and where to put our funds in order to have the finances we need to help out with a lot of the social justice concerns that are taking place in the world. In the days ahead we will need finances and the ability to mobilize people.

Jason says that in conjunction with the great economic revolution worldwide there will come revival in certain global "hotspots." Interestingly enough, many of these "hotspots" are also places that will see the greatest economic changes. Jason explains:

Revival is taking place, and we are going to continue to see it in China and in India because of what is going on over there. God is pouring out His Spirit there on an emerging group of people that are coming to the forefront. We need to understand that when God's Spirit falls, it falls on everybody, the righteous as well as the unrighteous. People start getting witty ideas for new inventions and other advances. They have visions. Something stirs up inside of them that gives them the confidence to believe they can change the world. We are seeing that in both these countries right now. It is happening also in New Zealand, Brazil, Australia, and

Ukraine. The peoples and economies of these nations will continue to emerge and their global influence will continue to grow.

A Message for the Philippines

A good example of the impact Jason is having in different parts of the world as a result of the spiritual insights he receives is the experience he had not long ago in the Philippines, where he influenced the weather as well as political leaders at the national level. He thought he was going there to work primarily with pastors. God had bigger plans. As Jason recalls:

> I was originally going to the Philippines as part of a team to work with over five hundred pastors. On the flight over, as the Lord would have it, I sat next to a gentleman who had the largest American company in the Philippines that employed Philippine citizens. As we talked, God began to give me insight into his life, what was going on personally, but also insight to what was going on in his company's management. When I look in the Spirit, He sometimes gives me insight into other people's lives. He shows me where their companies and organizations are, where they need to be, and practical steps of how to get there. He will put a plan and a strategy in place. So it feels a lot more like consultation, and I will do that whether I am dealing with a person, a business, a government, or a church. My goal is to help people deal with issues and actually see improvement take place.

During the flight the Lord began to touch this man's life. He also spoke to me and said, "I am going to open up the doors to the national government to you." I was in the country less than 12 hours when it began to happen. One thing led to another, until I found myself in a restaurant with the lady who owned it. She was serving our table when two other ladies came in and sat down, one of whom I had "seen" in prayer earlier that morning. I told her, "I saw you this morning," to which she replied, "I don't know you." I began to tell her what the Lord had shown me, relaying to her a lot of facts and details about her life to give credibility so that she would understand that God knew who she was. I told her the things that God wanted for her life and how to bring her into those things. She was completely touched. Nothing like that had ever happened to her before.

I then asked her, "Do you know any people in government?" I felt from the Lord that I was to ask right then and there because...

...God had given me a full one-page word for the nation of the Philippines.

God gave me a state of the union, where the nation was currently, where God wanted to bring it, and what the people needed to do to get to the place to turn things around.

She told me she had graduated from law school and had friends who were in the Philippine Senate. Then the lady who owned the restaurant told me that she knew one of the head senators, who actually was running for president at the time. The next thing I knew, I was on the phone with that gentleman, and I had not even been in the country 12 hours. I began to read off the word of the Lord to him. God touched him mightily right there on the phone. This political leader said to me, "This is everything I have been trying to tell these people. It is exactly what we need to be doing as a nation."

I thought it was pretty impressive watching how quickly God can open doors, but that was just the start. Immediately after I finished my phone conversation, a party of ten people entered the restaurant and sat down at the table right across from us. Everyone at our table perked up and I asked what was going on. "Those are high-ranking government officials," they told me. "Two of the people in that group help run the media for the entire nation."

The lady who owned the restaurant went over and talked to them, and they invited me over. I walked over and they said, "Please sit down. We hear that you have a word from God about our nation. We want to hear what God is saying over the Philippines right now." So I read the complete word to them. There were words that had to do with the economy, with the political environment, with society, and also with the environmental issues and the creation of the nation itself. They were really touched; the presence of God came over everybody. "Do you all understand this word?" I asked. They said yes. Then I said, "I want to pray for you," and they said, "Please do." So I had them all hold hands, government officials and people in the media, right in the center of this well-to-do restaurant, and the presence of God came in a very powerful way. I began to pray for wisdom for them that God would allow the righteous to begin to lead and decisions be brought forth to empower the whole nation.

Amazing things happened when we were in the Philippines. Less than 12 hours after entering the country I was talking with the decision makers of the nation, and an hour and a half later I was with some of the poorest people on the planet, in a place called Smokey Mountain. There we witnessed God doing numerous miracles, including three deaf children who had their hearing completely restored.

After that we flew to a nearby island and the Lord said to me, "I want you to pray that the resistance and the generational curses that have limited this nation and these people be broken." So we corporately repented for all the generational sins of the nation, and as we did so, winds began to blow into that place. Over 500 pastors were there, and more than 80 of them were healed miraculously with no one touching them, just because of the deep repentance that was taking place. God stretched out His hand and began to heal them. At the same time, a shift began to occur in the very weather patterns in the atmosphere. Before I left there, I said, "Because of the shift in powers that are taking place, in both the spiritual and geopolitical realms, within the next 24 hours there will be a significant earthquake in the Asia-Pacific rim." Twelve hours later a 5.8 magnitude earthquake hit Bali, Indonesia. It wasn't a bad earthquake, but it got everyone's attention.

The Lord wants to disciple the nations. He loves every nation and wants to see them come into the fulfillment and the fullness and the potential of what He has available for them.

Commissioned to Love

Jason Westerfield is a normal guy who is also a prototype of the new generation of people who know God. He walks in a high level of the supernatural realm and is both a witness to and an agent of miraculous works of God. Yet the focus of everything he does is *love*, because that is what the Lord commissioned him to do. As he explains:

When I was living in California prior to moving to my current home in New England, I had an amazing encounter with the Lord. In a vision the Lord walked up to me, put a sword over both of my shoulders, and said, "Jason, I am commissioning you to go out of this place and create cultures of love." Then He promised, "I will be with you." So I am very grateful for all the signs and the wonders and the miracles, for all the healings and people's lives being touched and restored, but the most important thing of all is whether there is more love in a place after I leave than there was before I came. Are the people more in love with God, more intimate with Him, and more open with Him than they were before? Is their love relationship with God stronger? Are they more in love with one another? Do they walk in deeper grace and compassion? These are the key questions—and the true standard for measuring success in ministry.

Paul said that without love we are nothing (see 1 Cor. 13:2). If we do not have love, it doesn't matter how gifted or talented we are or how much we walk in the supernatural realm. Apart from love, these things are meaningless. Some people say that faith is the most important. Faith *is* important, but faith works through love. God is love, and if we don't have love we are completely missing the point. As Christians we are to walk in love; we are to be clothed in love. We are the Lord's beloved, made in the image and likeness of love. So to be "normal" as a Christian means to walk with the Lord in love, allowing Him to make us lovely and enable us to love those around us.

Every believer who has intimacy with God can walk this way. The way of love is a believers' ministry, not a special persons' ministry, because we are all special to God and He loves us all. Reformation is coming. I believe that the defining characteristic of this new generation of Bible believers and followers of Jesus will be that walking in the supernatural will be *normal*. It will be the rule rather than the exception. More than ever before, believers will walk in an intimate and personal relationship with God. We will both hear and see what the Father is doing, and will join Him in His work. We will know who we are as sons and daughters of God, and will recognize the royalty in everyone, not just the few who move in healings, miracles, signs and wonders.

Are you normal? Then you are just the kind of person God is looking for. He's not interested in superstars. Jason Westerfield isn't a superstar; he just happens to have the only true "Superstar" living inside him. He just happens to believe the Bible; he just happens to hear from God; and he just happens to be...*normal*. If you want to enjoy greater intimacy with God and walk more deeply in the supernatural realm, learn to be yourself. Submit yourself to God. Trust in His Word and embrace His love for you. Let the Spirit of God make you normal—just as God has always intended for you to be.

Prayer of Impartation

Jason's testimony is an awesome example of living the normal, miraculous believer's life. He saw God talking to people in the Bible, and he simply asked if God would speak to him in the same way. Jason didn't follow a formula, he just sought God the best way he knew how and asked for what he saw in the Bible.

Let's ask God for what we see in the Bible:

Lord, I want to know you the way that David, Moses, and others knew you. I want to know you in intimate worship the way David did. I want to see you face-to-face the way Moses did when his face shined (see Exod. 33:11; 34:29).

Jesus, You said that Your followers would walk in greater miracles than You did on earth, and I want to walk in those miracles (see John 14:12-13). I want to see the dead rise, the sick healed, the lame walk (see John 11:1-44; Matt. 11:4-5).

God, give me a grid to understand the way that you work. Teach me how to walk out my supernatural faith. Help me to measure normal by how Jesus lived. Amen.

Jason shared that God enhanced his abilities. He wasn't born with a natural ability to understand physics and geometry, but God touched him, and these things come easily to Jason now. He also had an encounter that allowed him to understand that God loved him just the way he was. God loves you just the way that you are.

I'm going to pray that you receive an impartation from God that will usher you into a deeper realm of the supernatural.

In the name of Jesus, I release you into the Kingdom realm where the miraculous is normal. I impart supernatural learning—a quickening and acceleration of learning so that you will be able to conquer what you weren't able to learn before. You will comprehend matters that have previously been a mystery to you, and you will understand these things so well that you can teach them.

I release an authority over you to pray for those with blockages in their minds. You will break off generational curses, and your words will cause chromosomes to change and physical healings to take place. The Holy Spirit will touch those with ADD, ADHD, autism, and mental retardation. Total restoration will take place.

I release over you an ability to partner with the angels. You will sense the coming shifts of spiritual seasons and discern what God is doing in the earth. You will call leaders and nations into their God given destiny. Your words will call the promises of God into reality, breathe life into hopeless situations, and edify everyone who hears them.

You are a child of God—a son, a daughter of the King of kings. Everywhere that you go, you carry the power, authority, and influence of Heaven. You are the expression of Heaven on earth. God will use you to touch and disciple the nations. Your *normal* relationship with God will set the precedent for new believers. You will reproduce a generation of intimate worshipers of God who will walk in signs and wonders that declare the glory and faithfulness of God to all people.

For further information about Jason's ministry, please visit www.kingdomreality.com.

My Supernatural Experiences

_____

_____

_____

_____

_____

_____

_____

_____

_____

_____

_____

_____

SID ROTH'S IT'S SUPERNATURAL! AND MESSIANIC VISION
P.O. Box 1918
BRUNSWICK, GA 31521-1918

(912) 265-2500
(912) 265-3735 FAX

WEBSITE: WWW.SIDROTH.ORG EMAIL: INFO@SIDROTH.ORG

MESSIANIC VISION CANADA
SUITE 143
5929 L JEANNE D'ARC BLVD. ORLEANS,
ONTARIO K1C 7K2

EMAIL: CANADA@SIDROTH.ORG

In the right hands This Book will Change Lives!

Most of the people that need this message will not be looking for this book. To change their life you need to put a copy of this book in their hands.

> *But others (seeds) fell into good ground, and brought forth fruit, some a hundred-fold, some sixty-fold, some thirty-fold* (Matt. 13:3-8).

Our ministry is constantly seeking methods to find the good ground, the people that need this anointed message to change their life. Will you help us reach these people?

> *Remember this—a farmer who plants only a few seeds will get a small crop. But the one who plants generously will get a generous crop* (2 Cor. 9:6).

EXTEND THIS MINISTRY BY SOWING
3-BOOKS, 5-BOOKS, 10-BOOKS, **OR MORE TODAY**,
AND BECOME A LIFE CHANGER!

Thank you,

Don Nori Sr., Publisher
Destiny Image
Since 1982